Contents

Introduction	03
How to Use This Book	04
The Supplies	05
Getting Started	07
• *The Collection/Stash Box*	07
• *Introduction to the Visual Exercises*	08
• *Using Technology*	09
• *The Visual Exercises;*	12
1. Splitting Shapes	12
2. 30 Days of Cutting Stamps	13
3. Solid Shapes into Line Drawings	14
4. Mark Making	15
5. Collecting Textures	17
6. Photographs into Imagery	18
7. Drawings of Natural Objects	19
8. Representing Feelings	20
9. Line Studies	21
10. Rubbings	22
11. On Location Sketching	23
12. Mono Printing	24
13. Colour & Pattern Collage	26
14. Abstraction of an Object	28
15. What If?	30
16. What's Emerging?	31
Moving Forward	33
• *Principles versus Tools*	33
• *Contrast & Relationship*	35
• *The Door into the Picture World*	39
• *Balance*	41
• *Integration, Visual Bridges and The Elegant Choice*	43
How's it Going?	45
• *Take Time Out*	45
• *Using the Checklist*	45
• *Seeking Solutions & Making Decisions*	47
• *Some Rules of Thumb*	49
Going Deeper	50
• *Introduction*	50
• *Case Study 1 – It's all Academic*	51
• *Case Study 2 – Water*	53
• *The Writing Exercises;*	56
1. Free Association	57
2. Letter Writing	57
3. Location Writing	58
4. Visualising	58
5. Questioning	59
6. Colour Free Association	59
7. What's Emerging?	60
• *Re-visit and keep working*	61
Resources/Suppliers	62
Further Reading	63
About Us	64

Finding Your Own Visual Language | 01

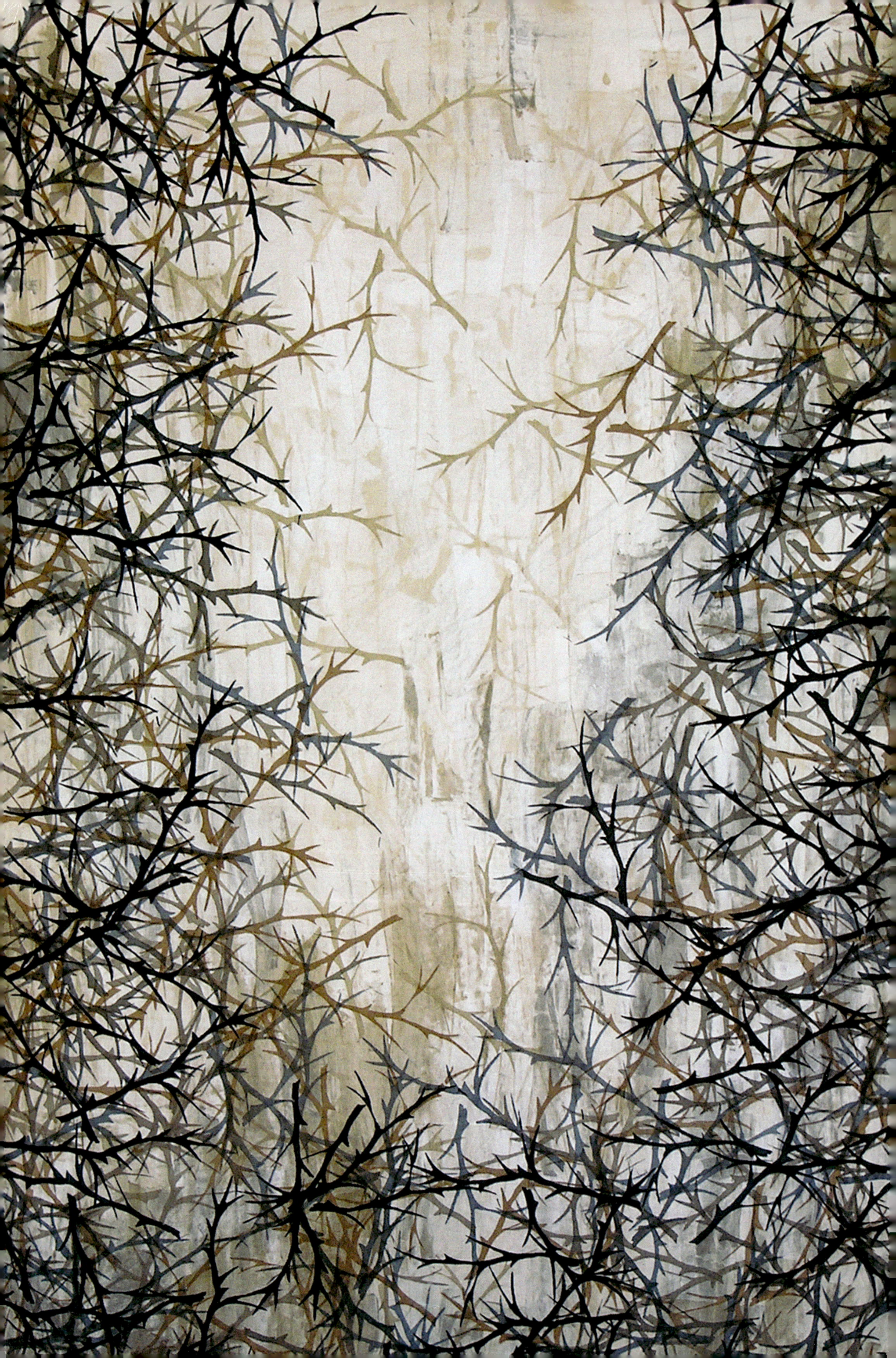

Introduction

There are many reasons you are holding this book. Could be curiosity. Could be you got it as a gift. But most of the time when someone reaches for a design book it's because they're feeling inadequate somehow. The desire exists to "make better work."

What does that mean – wanting to "make better work"? We've discussed it at length. The conclusions we've drawn are:

Better work might mean making work that gets exhibited. Or it could mean making work that's more satisfying. Or making work that demonstrates mastery over a series of techniques. But eventually it boils down to reaching a point in your process where what you create *feels right* – it's making work you want to share with the world. Making work you're proud of. It involves the development of Confidence - in yourself, in your process and in your end result. So that's what we want to talk about – the development of confidence on several levels.

We want to discuss technique and how important it is to practice, practice, practice when it comes to gaining mastery over technique. Without it, the work will never be as strong as it is once mastery is attained. But our interest isn't in refining specific technique. You can be a quilter or a collage artist or a photographer – explore whatever discipline appeals to you! No matter what your area of interest, time is required to develop mastery. It's a lifelong process. And it doesn't happen in a vacuum.

In the meantime, we propose four equally valuable areas for your consideration - each of which you will encounter as you develop and mature as an artist.

First: **How to Get Started**. Whether you're full of ideas or running on empty, how do you begin the process of designing?

And once you're underway: **How To Move Forward**. There are strategies to solve design problems. One of them is to understand the *Principles and the Language*. We'll explain the principles. We think we have a new approach to design terminology that makes it simpler and easier to understand. In addition to discussing Principles and Language, we want to talk about *Tools*. There are clear paths of analysis you can use when you need help, and one important aspect of strategy is to understand fully the tools you use to *build* your work.

But what if you get stuck? Everyone does now and then. Sometimes it's momentary and sometimes it's excruciatingly long and drawn out. The question we raise is **How's It Going?** The ironic answer? It's never an issue unless things aren't going well. If you realize you're stuck, then choose a strategy to evaluate the problem, contemplate the solutions, and make the needed changes to get going again.

Finally, there's the idea of **Going Deeper**. This means acknowledging the itchy niggling that happens when you want your work to be purposeful, or you're seeking specific *meaning* within your work. Some people refer to this as developing a surer artistic *Voice*. There are definitely exercises you can do – and ways of thinking you can cultivate to push through to a deeper place with your work.

All of this wraps around a key idea which is active during each stage of your process. It is the value of *intentional work*, or put quite simply – the value of INTENT. We define *intent* as "producing work you set out to produce, achieving in tangible form the idea you had in your head." No amount of reading or studying leads to intentional work *all* the time...but paying attention and Doing the Work leads to intentional work *more* of the time. And this, we believe, leads not only to satisfying work - it leads back to our start. The accomplishment of *better* work!

So let's begin.

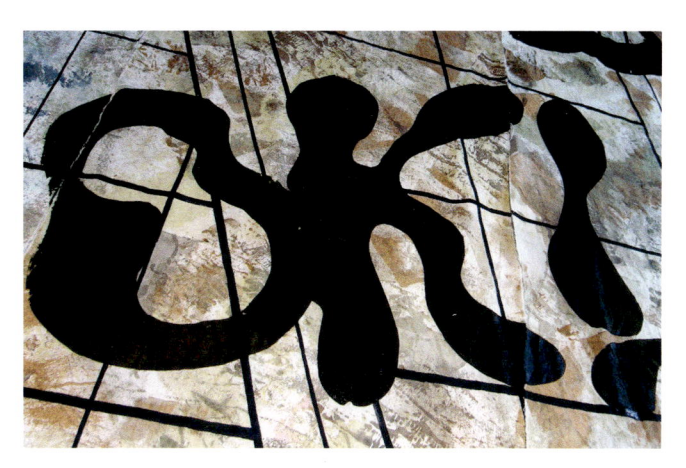

Work-in-progress, Amelia Garcia Leigh

**Left: *A sense of looking through*
 *(Leslie Morgan, work-in-progress)***

Finding Your Own Visual Language | 03

How to Use This Book

When we began brainstorming this book, we started - believe it or not - with what we DIDN'T want to do. For instance, we agreed we didn't want art speak, because so many people are confused by terminology. The English language is complicated enough.

We agreed we didn't want to do a color book - at least not as part of this book. Color rightly deserves an entire book to itself – which will be another project. In the meantime, you'll find these activities focus on black and white exercises because when color is eliminated the seduction of color is also eliminated. It's easier to "see" composition and analyze the principles discussed if color isn't permitted to interfere with the conversation.

We also agreed that we didn't want to be wordy or intimidating. This didn't mean we had a desire to dumb down ideas, principles or tools. Design concepts are valid, rich with possibility, and inextricably rooted in human response to environment. They just are. Artists have no control over them. But we can learn the principles and then use them to our advantage.

We did agree that every principle or tool or strategy can be described simply and practiced regularly. So this shared belief is the underpinning of our book.

We've written it in four sections, which are basically about…

- Getting started

- Continuing on

- What to do when you get stuck, and then:

- How to delve deeper into your own Self if the desire to do so arises.

You might consider reading straight through from cover to cover as a way of becoming acquainted with the ideas. Or you can jump to the spot that addresses a need right now. Either strategy will work, but getting an overview by reading the whole book is probably useful early in your practice of the concepts.

We've provided many more exercises than you'll choose to complete. That was deliberate. If you start with exercises that appeal to you, it will be fun to do them, which is important. Other exercises can stand in waiting. An idea that isn't appealing right now may be just the trick a year or two out.

Which is part of our message. This is a guide to accompany you on your journey as an artist. Study it to learn the language and then refer to it whenever you need a brush up. Stuck? Get us out and run down the checklist. Sorting around for new ideas? Read or re-read the section on Going Deeper. The main thing? Keep working. Gather the supplies together so you have them on hand. Like the spices and seasonings you keep in the kitchen cabinet, these tools exist for your use at a moment's notice.

So enjoy yourself. But get going!

Supplies

Everything on this list is easy to find and inexpensive to acquire. We list resources on page 62 and have tried to identify items in both North American and British/European terms. And by the way, this goes for the spelling too. We haven't attempted to put the book entirely into North American or British English, but left the spelling according to whoever wrote each particular section. A true transatlantic collaboration!

Specific supplies are detailed for each exercise, but as an overview, you'll need:

- High quality black paper (not construction paper, which doesn't cut easily with a knife). Canson or Mi Tientes are good brands
- A pad of good tracing paper
- Torn pages from color magazines (start a stash)
- Glue stick
- Bottle glue for paper
- Clear, sticky cellophane tape
- Masking or decorators tape
- Sharp bladed craft knife (an Exacto or similar)
- A cutting surface or mat
- Scissors
- Plain white paper for backgrounds and some of the texture exercises
- Several black markers – any brand. A variety of tips and widths is good
- Black and white crayons – varied sizes – the fat children's crayons make excellent marks
- Black charcoal, butcher's pencils – other mark making implements you encounter unexpectedly
- Black India ink
- Black and white Tempera paint or Acrylic Paint
- A small piece of flat heavy plastic, acrylic sheet, glass or a ceramic tile.
- Mark-making tools such as foam rollers and brushes, bristle brushes, scrapers (an old credit card), old forks, old combs etc.
- An assortment of brushes from a tiny tip to a wide housepainter's brush
- A notebook/sketchbook – this is a working notebook for samples, notes and ideas, plans for "what next"

Various exercises may request or suggest other miscellaneous items like appropriated tools: sponges, a potato masher, the edge of a piece of Plexiglas. You can add these to your basic supplies as the need or impulse arises. Equally, artists with specific textile skills may prefer to use black and white fabric backed with an iron-on fusible product to complete some of the exercises.

Photograph by James Gillham

A collection of sea urchins (photograph by John Chalker)

Getting Started

How many times have you bought an instructional book and absolutely loved it? Looking endlessly at the beautiful pictures? Reading and re-reading the text? Hmmm. But you never got off the mark in the studio. Reading and looking became the activity rather than the making the book was written to inspire? It happens.

Maybe it's because you don't know where to start. That's not uncommon. It takes practice to learn to generate ideas worth interpreting as a work of art. Or perhaps you have ideas you'd like to explore, but you don't have a clue when it comes to process – the actual working out of the idea through technique. That's a frustrating situation and one only overcome by working. Perhaps patience will be required because you haven't mastered the skills you need to realize your ideas. Everyone faces that problem, too. The only way through it is, again – doing the work. Fretting because you don't know how to do what you need to do, when you could be getting started and doing it, is a huge waste of both energy and time.

So, try to get over yourself and pick up the brush or the pen. We think of it as being a grown up. Do what needs to be done.

The Collection/Stash Box
No matter what your interests, it's a good idea to create a Collection or "Stash" Box. You may already have it underway and not even know it. Anyone who has torn out a magazine picture because the colors or the patterning were seductive, or picked up shells on the beach, or a cast-off from the street, has the idea. Our personal collection of inspirations is what sets our work apart from everyone else.

If your own odd assortment of items is scattered around the studio – or on the ledge of the kitchen window, that's okay. Just add another dimension to the collecting and acquire images and objects deliberately. Keep your eyes open and accumulate the various riff and raft in a single box. This makes it available for inspiration any time you need the help. You are NOT accumulating with a purpose in mind. Rather, you are accumulating for the love or allure of the object or image. Time will tell how those objects and images influence your work, or make their appearance in it.

And don't put everything in a beautifully crafted notebook or journal. This is not a prejudice against journals and notebooks – writing is an important part of the process, as you will see. But it's not unusual to find that the notebook becomes the artwork, rather than playing a secondary role in its creation. It's also easier to sort through a box than it is to review notebooks (or tear pages from one), so give the Stash Box serious consideration.

Finding Your Own Visual Language | 07

Spirals by Leslie

Spirals by Claire

Spiral by Jane

The Visual Exercises
Personalities differ. Some people can jump into an open-ended experience and love the unknowing. Others HATE it when they don't know what's going to happen. They are more comfortable with a general idea of outcome. The exercises listed here are adaptable. They suit either way of working.

For instance, if you want to generate loads of raw visual material, pick any exercise that sounds like fun and do it. In one version of this book as a class, participants choose ten exercises and complete ten variations on each theme. Each piece of the hundred or so images they produce isn't immediately useful, but the experience of generating so many images at once is HUGELY useful. It demonstrates the value of multiple choices, but also the benefit of bountiful raw material - to consult and access for other projects.

On the other hand, if you prefer to have a goal for your exercises, then choose an image as a starting point. The image provides visual reference. Inspiration can come from:

- A picture: a plant in the garden, the rolling hills of a landscape, a magazine image. Close ups may be easier to work with than a landscape. Trying the image out will indicate whether it's a choice you want to pursue.
- An actual object: a leaf, a human hand, a stone, a snippet of ethnic embroidery.
- A texture: rug canvas, a close-up photo of grasses (yes, the inspiration can overlap categories…) the pebbly surface of a shingle beach.
- A shape: a circle, a spiral, a diamond, a square etc.

And by the way, don't be intimidated by the idea that a shape has been 'done'. Spirals, crosses, squares and the like are all symbols as old as humankind. No one owns these images. They are part of our collective unconscious. If one of them resonates, and cries out to be used – do it. Your goal will then be to use the image in a way that is uniquely your own.

As examples - which you'll find illustrate the text - we've chosen a leaf, a circle, and a piece of rug canvas. Their inclusion demonstrates the possibilities for various types of images. Don't make life hard for yourself! Choose a simple, recognizable image to start. Once you're underway you can keep going with the image or abandon it and switch to something else. No one is grading. It's up to you. The main thing is to choose.

If you've chosen the open-ended route, follow the exercises and the variations as they are written. If you select an object or an image to use as your starting point, you may need to adapt the exercise to fit your choice. Not all exercises adapt readily to a pre-conceived object or idea. If the exercise doesn't seem to be working, set it aside and choose another one.

One more general bit of advice before you begin: Keep it Simple.

Illustrating the various exercises too literally or as complicated designs might eventually be valuable, but when you are beginning simple is good. **If you are having trouble with an exercise, ask yourself this question: How can I simplify?**

08 | Finding Your Own Visual Language

Technology

Technology is great. Here are some basic ideas concerning the access of technology – based on your experience you may be able to do quite a bit more than what we suggest here. There are four tools that are useful no matter which of the exercises you complete - the photocopy machine, the computer, clear transparency film (also known as acetate) and windowing 'L's.

The Photocopy Machine

Home copiers are relatively inexpensive, but copy shops make playing on a machine even easier, and affordable. Some computer printers do double duty by allowing you to copy, reduce and enlarge without going through the computer itself. Consider these possibilities:

- Enlarge the designs you've created. Not just once, but several times – think BIG.
- Reduce the designs you've created. Not just once, but several times – think tiny.
- Isolate portions of the design and work strictly with the detail. This might be after greatly enlarging or reducing the image. Or you can cut out a part of the original design and play with it.
- Make multiple copies of the same design and generate a repeating pattern. OR cut out the same part of multiple images and reassemble the pieces into a repeating pattern.

The Computer

Computers and programs vary, of course, but most computers have simple photo programs capable of altering visual imagery by changing colors, size and style of design elements. Computers allow images to be tessellated, flipped, shaded, bent and distorted. You may also have a program provided by the digital camera you own – so investigate the possibility of using the camera program to alter images.

There are usually two choices to get your imagery on to the computer – scanning an image directly into a computer program, or photographing the design work digitally, and downloading the photos into a photo program. Explore the potential of the programs you already own, and then consider purchasing a simple program to expand your options. KidPix is a brand name program designed for children – but any adult would love playing with the design options. Powerpoint, Photoshop, Picasa (from Google), Apple Works and Keynote (Mac) are simple programs that are easy to learn.

Uninspiring squiggles (created with a fine brush and India ink) turn into cruel hooks and barbs when enlarged several times on the photocopier

The hooks and barbs turn into very personal barbed wire imagery

A squiggly circle, drawn with brush and ink...

The squiggly circle is manipulated on the computer in one way...

...and another way

Finding Your Own Visual Language | 09

Having fun with Photo Booth on the Mac

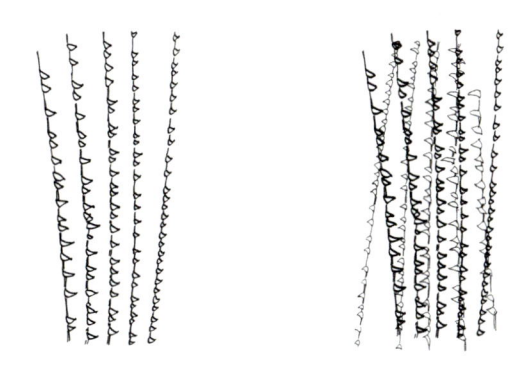

Mark-making in the style of 'thorns', multiplied using an acetate overlay

Using several acetates to explore design overlays

Acetates/Transparencies
Acetate is clear plastic film designed to be printed by photocopiers and printers. The sheets feed through the machine just like paper. Clear transparencies allow you to "audition" design ideas including:

- multiple combinations of elements
- placement and orientation
- size and shape contrasts and similarities

as well as other potential relationships related to composition. You can draw directly on to acetate with India ink or markers. It is one of the most useful tools in your toolbox, and recycled acetate sheets are inexpensive when purchased by the box.

Windowing Out, Cropping & Selecting
Sometimes a piece of design work, imagery or work-in-progress doesn't cut the mustard as a whole. Cropping and\or selecting elements from the whole can often yield great results. The low-tech approach involves the use of 'L' shaped cards (see below). These are moved around to find 'windows' of potential. Alternatively, take a photograph of the design/piece and use the computer to crop or select specific elements. So, whilst something may not work as a whole, it may yield several small, perfect compositions.

Okay, so there's some general guidance and things to think about. Let's take a look at the practical exercises.

Finding Your Own Visual Language | 11

Visual Exercise 1
Splitting Shapes

Split-shape circles and leaves

Supplies
- Black paper
- White paper/your sketchbook
- Scissors or a knife – whatever works best for you
- Glue stick or bottled glue
- Optional: Work with black cloth backed with fusible web instead of black paper

The Goal: to split recognizable shapes into parts, which are then reassembled with the cut portions slightly separated or pulled apart.

The Method
1. Choose a rectangle, a triangle, a circle, a square, etc. Start with something simple.
2. Cut the shape into at least three pieces or as many as you like. Choose to cut in one direction only (horizontally, vertically, diagonally) or cut in several directions.
3. Now reassemble the cut pieces. Remember; nothing can be added or taken away. You choose the spacing between the individual parts, but the 'visual integrity' of the shape is important to maintain. In other words, if you started with a square, the reassembled pieces must resemble a square at the end of the re-assembly.
4. When you're happy with the arrangement, glue the pieces onto white paper.
5. Do 6 to 8 samples of the exercise.

Review
Consider:
- A single image can be altered significantly depending on the placement of individual parts when you glue the cut up shapes to the background paper. Play with placement before you glue the paper to the background permanently.
- When do you lose the shape completely?
- When is the shape more interesting (or less interesting) based on spacing and number of cut pieces?
- Try enlarging or reducing the shapes on the photocopier/computer.
- Try photocopying the shape several times and playing with pattern repeat arrangements (this can be fun to do with two shapes).

Claire Higgott's quilt ('Illusion'), made as a result of the split shape exercise

12 | Finding Your Own Visual Language

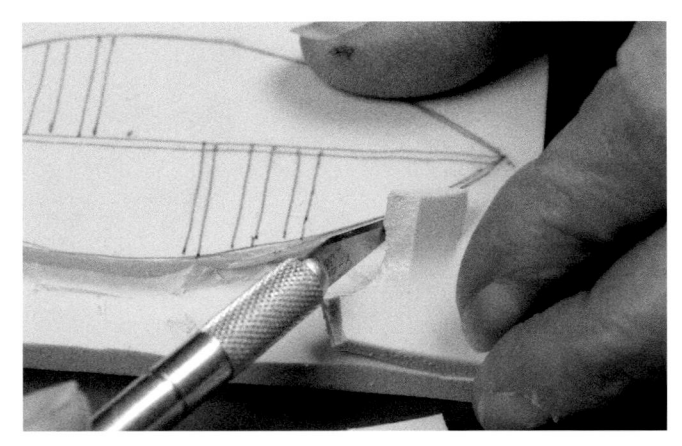

Cutting away the edge of the eraser with a craft knife

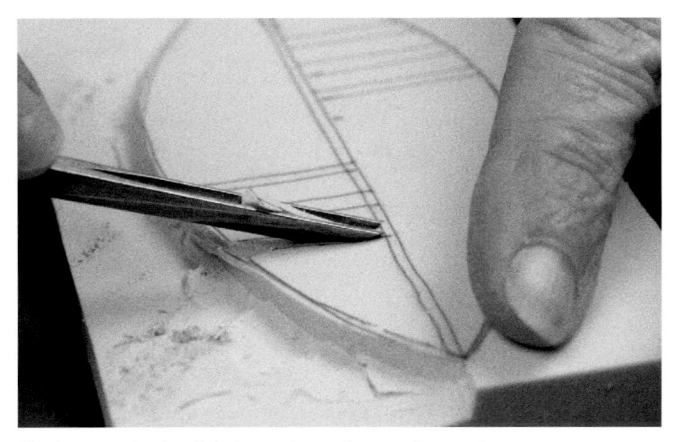

Cutting out the leaf design using a lino-cutting tool

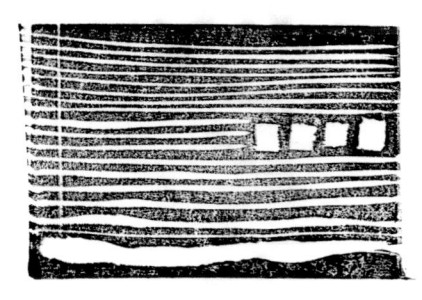

A print of a linear design cut from a large rubber stamp

A simple rubber stamp image printed within a circular template (cut and printed by Jeanie McBride)

Visual Exercise 2
30 Days of Cutting Stamps

Supplies
- 30 erasers (gum or white plastic erasers are easiest to cut)
- Craft knife with a sharp, pointed blade (such as an Exacto knife)
- Pencil

Optional:
- Plexiglas pieces and permanent adhesive to form the individual stamps into larger printing blocks
- Linoleum cutters if you have them

The Goal: to explore the possibilities of stamping as a design tool.

The Method
Cut one stamp eraser every day for a month. If this isn't appealing, cut six stamps during one sitting, six during the next and so forth.

Variations On the Theme
- If you have chosen an image as inspiration, create that image as six or more stamps.
- Stamp erasers in black paint on white paper in full-page, repeated patterns. Do several pages of combinations. These will be useful raw material for other exercises.
- Enlarge and reduce some of the pages of printing. Reduce one page so that it is really small. Enlarge another page so that it is REALLY BIG.

Review
Consider:
- Does one stamp printed in multiples make the individual image more interesting? Sometimes the stamp has potential to be a completely different image when used as a multiple image.
- Do alternating stamps make interesting patterns? Which combinations have the most potential for use later? Not all combinations are equally interesting visually.

Finding Your Own Visual Language | 13

Card cut-outs of Camelia leaves

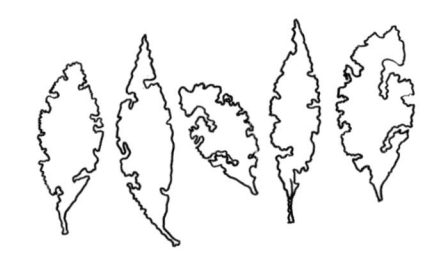

The same leaves, traced as outlines

Outlines of leaves, cut from paper created in Visual Exercise 9 (Line Studies)

A circle, traced from one created in Visual Exercise 1 (Splitting Shapes), decorated with a simple line design

Visual Exercise 3
Solid Shapes into Line Drawings

Supplies
- Black paper or the black paper cut outs you created for Exercise No. 1
- Craft knife or scissors if you intend to make new shapes
- Glue stick or bottled glue if you are creating new shapes
- A pencil or marker
- Good quality tracing paper

The Goal: to alter flat, solid shapes by converting them into line drawings.

The Method
1. Lay the black paper shape mounted on white paper on the worktable.
2. Position the tracing paper over the black paper shape.
3. Trace the outlines of the image onto the tracing paper with the marker or pencil.
4. Complete 6 – 8 examples.

Variations On the Theme
- Embellish the line drawing by adding detail or patterning within the lines.
- If you have completed Mark Making Exercise No. 4 or Texture Exercise No. 5, consider combining them with this exercise by using photocopies of these textures or marks, and tracing/cutting out shapes. The textures and marks will create the patterning for you.
- Enlarge and reduce your drawings on the photocopier/printer.

Review
Consider:
- Are the line drawings more interesting if the line is fatter or thinner?
- Are the images more interesting if they are filled in with patterning?
- Does enlarging or reducing the line drawing make it more or less interesting?
- How well do the line drawings work with the original shapes?

Visual Exercise 4
Mark Making

A leaf shape created with a brush and India ink

Another leaf, drawn with an italic felt-tip pen

A circluar mark made with a wax crayon

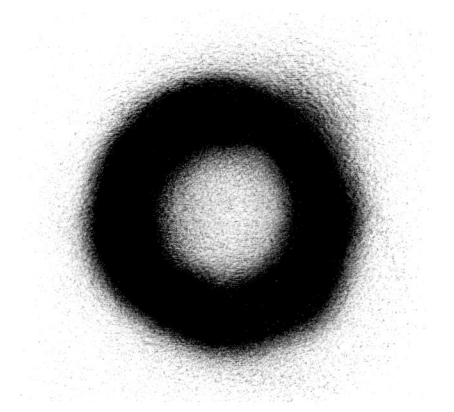

A circular mark made using spray paint

Supplies
- Pens, pencils and other markers
- An assortment of brushes
- Other tools to use with paint/ink; old credit cards, rollers, syringes, twigs (chewed or otherwise), grass heads, chopsticks, scrapers etc. (and there's always your fingers)
- A range of paints/inks from Black Tempera paint, India ink or black dye dissolved in water (different consistencies will yield different results)
- White paper - try this activity with a variety of different papers. The paper selected will generate different results (photocopy paper, lining paper, sketch-book or watercolor paper, blotting paper etc.)
- A container for water

The Goal: to explore the potential of the mark and the possibilities for using marks in quantity. Forget ideas about composition etc. This is all about engaging with the activity and seeing what happens in terms of creating marks. Banish expectations on 'finished' work. You are playing, experimenting, looking and learning.

The Method
The best approach to this exercise is rather freewheeling – set a timer, for example, or mark until an entire page is filled. Complete these samples:
1. A page of random dots.
2. A page filled more carefully with dots – so that the dots generate a pattern.
3. A page using one or more of the tools to make marks.
4. A page using the brushes and black paint to make marks.
5. Change the pressure you apply to the tool as you mark – will the marks change too?
6. A page made completely with your eyes shut.
7. Try different types of paint or ink; different consistencies will yield different results.
8. Complete at least 6 to 10 pages of marks.

Finding Your Own Visual Language | 15

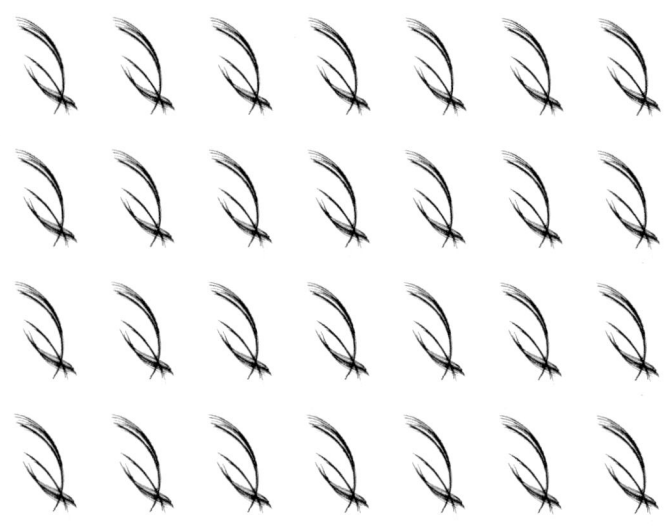

A leaf, reduced and repeated

Maggie explores large-scale tools and marks. Elements from the whole were later reduced and enlarged

Variations On The Theme
- Mark to music.
- Mark a page every morning for a week – will the pages vary greatly?
- Mark outdoors.
- Photocopy the pages of marks, enlarging and reducing them. A change of scale can dramatically alter the look of the marks you made.
- Mark with much larger tools such as a broom or a great big brush.
- Put the paper on the floor (lay down newspaper first!) or the ground and tie your tools to the end of canes and mark from a greater distance.
- Try working with a different physical focus; work only from your wrist, then try and work only from your elbow and then try and work from your shoulder.
- Try taping the paper on to a board and working on the vertical rather than the flat.
- Try working on smaller pieces of paper.
- Try mark-making with a pen whilst sitting as a passenger in a car (great on bumpy roads).

Review
Consider:
- How wide can a line be before it's no longer perceived as a line and becomes a shape?
- Do some of your marks remind you of anything; people, trees, fish, plants, leaves, barbs, hooks, chimneys etc. Think about the implication of this; you don't have to be able to draw to get the essence of a thing.
- Is a style merging, a favorite line/mark, a way of working that resonates with you? If so, do more - build on it.

Lines made with an italic ink pen (wide nib, used badly). These lines are almost shapes

16 | Finding Your Own Visual Language

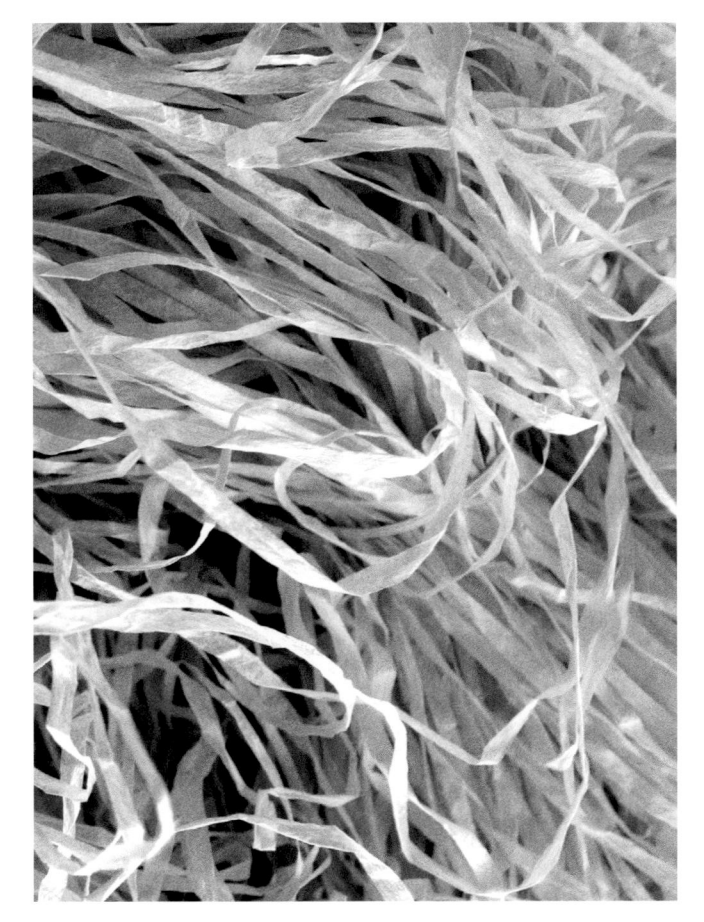

Visual Exercise 5
Collecting Textures

Supplies
- White paper or heavier cardstock
- Bottled glue
- An assortment of anything you think might be interesting. Heavily textured fabric like burlap or raffia, seeds, beans, pasta, rice, stones or pebbles, window screening, gravel, thick and thin paints, thick gels with sand or beads mixed in, paper surfaces with texture, paper stitched on the machine
- The photocopy machine or computer scanner

The Method
1. Create texture samples by gluing individual objects onto the paper or cardstock. Remember, one grain of rice is not very interesting, but rice packed onto a three inch square is no longer rice – it is a textural surface or pattern.
2. Most samples don't need to be any bigger than 3 or 4 inches in each direction.
3. If glueing grains of rice, salt etc. sounds tedious, scatter your textural items on black or white paper and photograph the result, or use the scanner.
4. This is an ongoing collection, but start with ten samples.

Variations On The Theme
- Photocopy the samples and enlarge or reduce them.
- Cut photocopies up and re-combine them. Photocopy again.
- Enlarge a texture so that it is no longer recognizable as what it was originally.
- Make a repeated pattern using squares or other shapes cut from the photocopies of texture.
- Hand color one of the pages to play with value and color as an option.

Review
Consider:
- Some elements may actually make worthwhile patterns glued in specific combinations.
- Some elements may not "make the final cut" – this is a case of an idea sounding a lot cooler than it is when translated into reality!

A close-up of raffia

To mimic the grid of a canvas, a yarn weaving was copied on to acetate and laid over the original

Salt sprinkled on to black paper...& reversed on the computer

Finding Your Own Visual Language | 17

A photograph of a Prayer plant

A line drawing from the Prayer plant image

A photograph of dessicated remains in a glass bowl

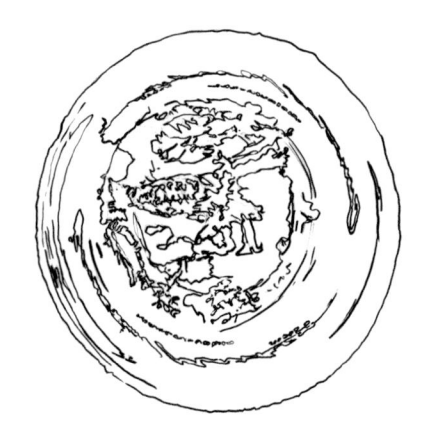

A tracing of the glass bowl photograph

Visual Exercise 6
Photographs Translated into Imagery

Supplies
- A digital camera OR a one time use color or b/w camera
- Processing ability – either on your own computer system or through a retail processing center

The Goal: the camera has the ability to capture specific qualities or unique perspectives of a subject. These photos are useful when translated as design elements.

The Method
1. Take 24 photographs with some appealing characteristic. The appeal is by its nature, an individual issue.
2. Consider making some portion of the images close up shots. Seek out shape or form, or texture. Overall shots can also be cropped later. Consider shooting from odd angles – get underneath, right on top and so forth.
3. Print six or eight of the images for additional study.

Variations On the Theme
- Turn color shots into b/w shots on the computer if you have those skills.
- Think about the light. Light plays an important part in how any photograph will look. Take an entire series of photos of shadows only. The potential to use these images as the basis for an abstract series is terrific.
- Photocopy colored photos so they become black and white images.
- Crop photocopies or the actual photo to isolate particular qualities.
- Choose one or more of the images, which could be drawn by hand or traced with tracing paper, and complete that variation.

Review
Consider:
- How does an image change when parts of it are enlarged or isolated? Is the abstract quality more interesting than the original, overall image?
- How does the line drawn version of the image compare to the original photographic image? Try not to judge your drawing skill!
- Remember to simplify.

18 | Finding Your Own Visual Language

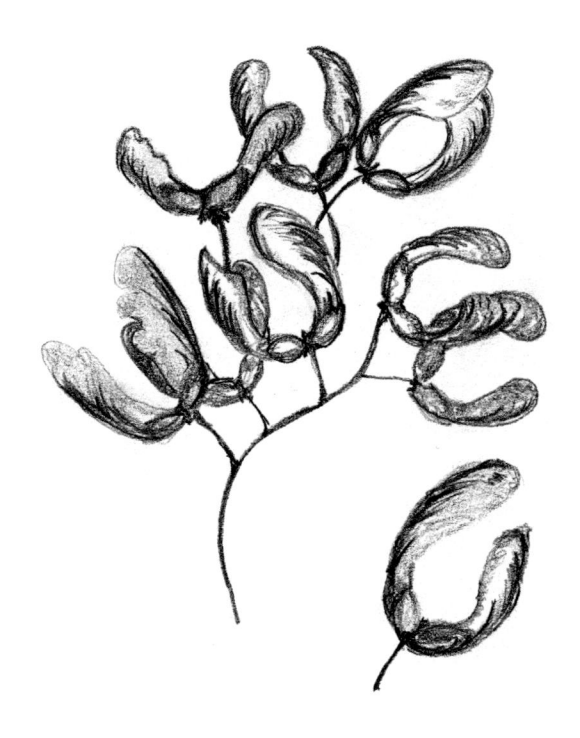

A detailed drawing of a sycamore seed

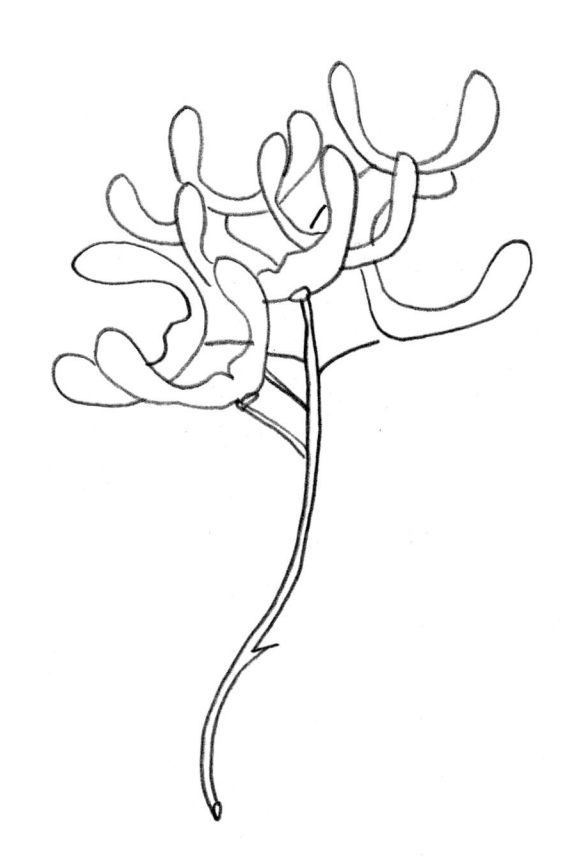

An outline drawing of the same sycamore seed

Visual Exercise 7
Detail Drawings of Natural Objects

Supplies
- Pencil or marker
- White paper
- Black paper and white chalk
- A series of natural objects – shells, stones, bark, seedpods, fish scales, a vegetable (try an artichoke or a pineapple)

The Goal: a detail drawing is a close up drawing. The goal is to study texture and form through the drawing exercise. Studies prove that human beings can draw an object by looking at it whilst drawing – using one continuous line. Referred to as contour drawing, this is an intuitive approach, and spontaneous. It is not a studied or educated approach to drawing fundamentals.

The Method
1. Choose an object for the study.
2. Try this first approach to drawing; put your pencil or marker to the paper and draw the object while you are looking at it – without looking at the paper.
3. Now try a second approach; draw the subject 'normally' (refer to the object whilst also referring to your drawing of it).
4. Move on to try a third approach; draw a portion of the object to get detail – this time study the surface of the object closely.
5. Finally, try drawing or sketching to a time limit: 10 seconds, 30 seconds, 1 minute or 5 minutes. Setting a time limit can help with procrastination and free you up.

Variations On the Theme
- Would another sort of drawing tool generate a different result?
- Try drawing or even painting a detail with ink and brush. Would one tool be more suited to re-creating the object's surface than another?
- Try five versions of the drawing using different tools. What about creating the image with a series of dots – placed closer to indicate shading and further to create open space.
- Copy – enlarge and reduce.

Review
Consider:
- It's easy to get an idea "stuck" in your head as having to look a particular way. Variations on this exercise encourage you to reconsider the idea from several vantage points.
- Your general drawing may not please you, but this is why the enlargements can be useful, allowing isolation and study of one or more areas of the drawing.
- Cutting up a photocopy of the drawing may be another way to push through to an image you want to reproduce or use in actual artwork.

Finding Your Own Visual Language

Exploring 'anger'

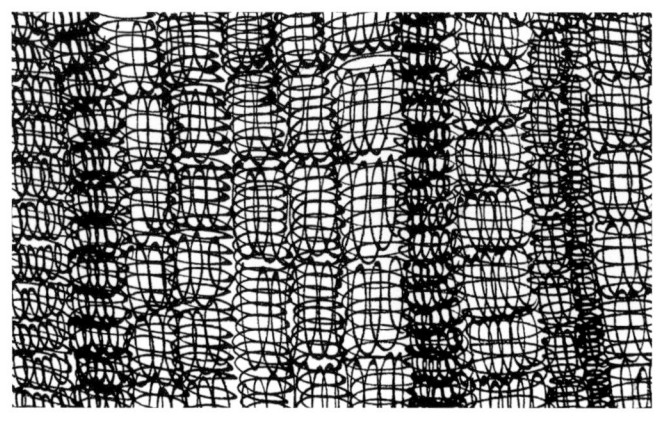

Exploring 'confusion'

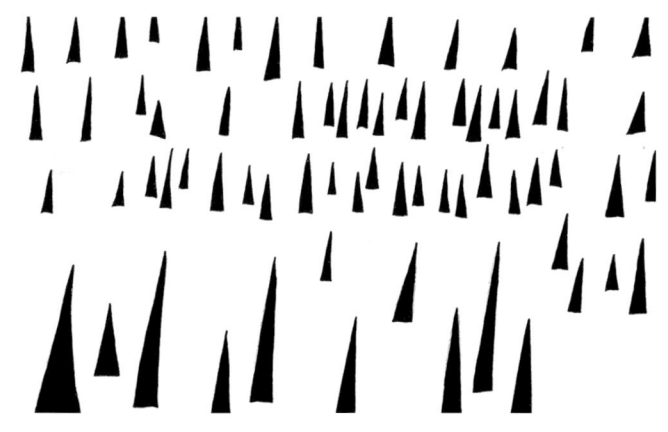

Exploring 'spiteful'

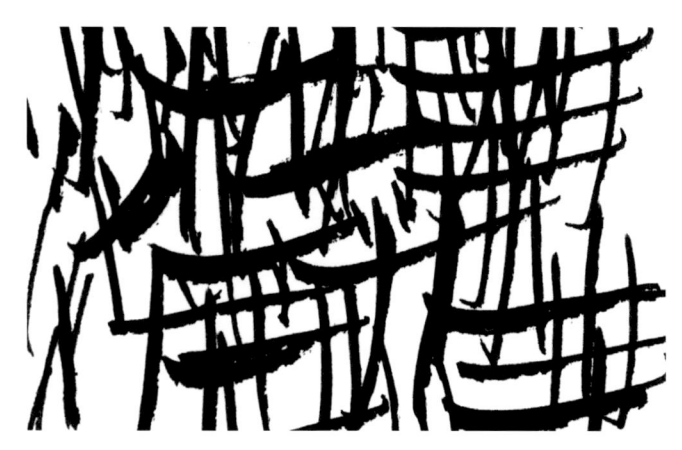

Exploring 'anxiety'

Visual Exercise 8
Representing Feelings

Supplies
- Black paper
- White paper
- Scissors or craft knife
- Glue stick or bottled glue
- Pens and markers

The Goal: to explore the potential for psychological or emotional qualities to be translated into a visual form.

The Method
1. Make a series of cut-outs (shapes or lines) representing emotions. For example:
   - Joy
   - Sorrow
   - Boredom
   - Anger
   - Balance – even temper
   - Confusion
2. Glue the shapes down on white paper and name them.
3. Repeat the exercises, but switch to using pens, pencils, brushes, etc.
4. Explore line as well as shape.

Variations On the Theme
- Use white chalk or marker on black paper backgrounds.
- Do the exercise again a week later. Do the images change?
- Don't label the shapes. Ask someone you know to identify the emotion being represented.

Review
Consider:
- Emotions are universal. If someone else can identify the emotion you represented with a shape or a line, that will open up some conversation.
- Working with this exercise is a taste of how to work abstractly. Other exercises address abstraction more specifically, but giving an emotion or an idea visual form is at the heart of the abstracting process.

These lines were drawn in the empty spaces of a plastic grid (a sink liner), using a wide-nib italic ink pen

Leaf as line...and reversed on the computer

Squiggly lines, over-laid with an acetate copy as a grid

The same squiggly line grid, reduced and tiled

Visual Exercise 9
Line Studies

Supplies
- Paper - an assortment of different papers, since the paper generates different results (photocopy paper, lining paper, sketch-book or watercolor paper, blotting paper etc.)
- Ink/paint/dye – India ink, tempera paint etc.
- Brushes – an assortment is good
- Pens - different types of nib and nib-widths, felt pens, fat marker pens etc.
- Pencils - soft leads and hard leads, big fat carpenters' pencils, grease pencil, etc.

The Goal: to explore the power of a line and the nature of a line versus a dot or a shape. Note: lines do not have to be straight.

The Method
1. Make a page of lines without thinking – fill the page.
2. Create a page with more forethought – do the lines "mean" something?
3. Use three different tools to generate distinctly different lines.
4. Make lines with cut paper and glue them down. The line quality of cut paper is quite different from a drawn line. Do four samples.

Variations On the Theme
- Draw lines to music.
- Draw lines standing up. Or use your whole arm instead of just your wrist.
- Enlarge and reduce the lines.
- Cut up enlarged or reduced photocopies and reconfigure them. Do shapes emerge from the line studies when they are combined as multiples?

Review
Consider:
- How wide can a line be, before it is no longer perceived as a line and becomes a form?
- If you make lines when you are nervous or upset, how are the lines influenced by your mood?
- If you listen to music are the lines obviously influenced by what you hear?

Finding Your Own Visual Language | 21

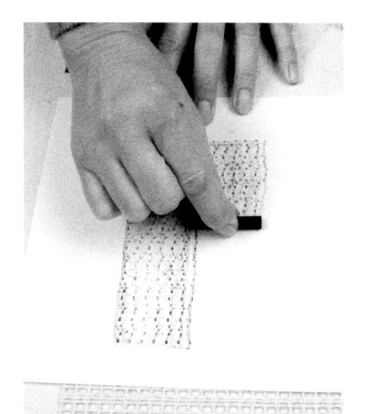

Taking a rubbing of rug canvas, using a wax crayon

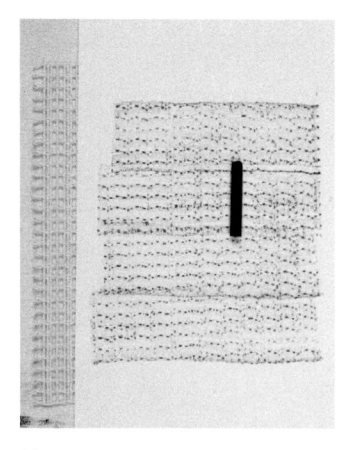

The completed rubbing

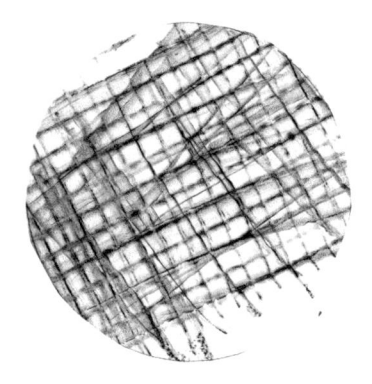

A rubbing of rug canvas cut into a circle

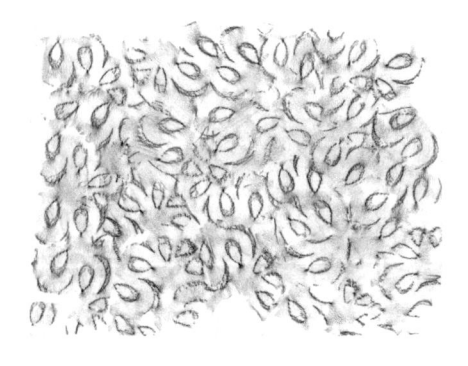

Multiple rubbings of a wooden printing block

Visual Exercise 10
Rubbings

Supplies
- Black crayons, charcoal or pastel sticks which can be rubbed over a surface using the entire length
- White paper – lightweight paper may work better than heavy paper

The Goal: to acquire a series of found images and textures from the world around you.

The Method
1. Work indoors or out of doors.
2. Look for surfaces with texture – old doors, metal plates, flooring, the side walk, tree bark – be open to ideas/triggers.
3. Put white paper on top of the textured surface and rub the side of the crayon or pastel or charcoal over the surface. The best image may be obtained by rubbing in one direction rather than back and forth. Experiment to figure this out.
4. Spray charcoal images with hair spray to "set" the charcoal and keep it from smudging.

Variations On the Theme
- Try different crayons/implements on the same surface. One may suit the surface better than another.
- Use black paper and white crayon. Or a white paper with colored crayons. Do be aware that black on white usually copies readily, while colors may present reproduction problems.

Review
Consider:
- The hardness or softness of the crayon or other implement affects the crispness of the rubbed image. If you are computer savvy you can scan the image and sharpen it up on the computer screen.
- Substituting a roller and paint for the crayon produces yet another variation from the rubbing. Old tin ceiling panels underneath white fabric make wonderful patterns when paint is rolled over them. Keep the tools dry and use as little paint as possible to maintain clarity of the image.
- How many other ways can you adapt the idea of rubbings?

Visual Exercise 11
On Location Sketching

A sketch of electrical cables in the street

Ruth sketches the lines of the wisteria trunk

Supplies
- White paper – a pad might be best so you have support for your sketching
- Pens, markers

The Goal: to expand horizons by using the world around you as resource material.

The Method
1. Visit a museum, the park or sit in a coffee shop and observe the environment and atmosphere around you.
2. Choose an object and study it. Observe:
   - Pattern
   - Texture
   - Shape
   - Relationship of parts
   - Themes
3. If you aren't interested in an object, observe the scene around you - people or activities - and make sketches of those elements in the environment.

Variations On the Theme
- If you are looking at people can you make a few lines only – representative of their demeanor? Without getting too detailed?
- Think about different styles of designing. See the discussion on pages 35 and 37 for more information on stylistic interpretations, if it's a new idea. Draw the same object, but use more than one approach stylistically.
- Try sketching a subject within a time limit: 10 seconds, 30 seconds, 1 minute or 5 minutes. Setting a time limit can help you focus on catching the essence of something and free you up generally.
- Instead of On Location Sketching consider On Location Looking! Just observe the world around you, or the object at hand for several concentrated minutes. See how much you can file away in your brain – texture, form, color. Go home and reproduce what you saw from memory.

Review
Consider:
- Sometimes we're so preoccupied with "being" we don't notice much about the world around us. This is a great exercise if you like the notion of getting outside of yourself.
- People who make a career of art revisit topics, objects and themes over and over again during the course of their lives. Degas never got tired of drawing dancers and Chuck Close has never tired of representing what he calls Big Heads – faces generated in a variety of styles and media. Don't ever think you've done enough with an idea or form. There is always something else to be learned from observing it.

Finding Your Own Visual Language

Applying black Tempera paint to a piece of sheet plastic

Scraping out marks using an old fork

Lay the painted plastic on to paper, then lift it off (you could print on to cloth instead of paper)

Visual Exercise 12
Mono Printing

Supplies
- Black and white paper or card
- Black and white Tempera or Acrylic paint
- An assortment of brushes; try foam and/or bristle
- A foam roller
- An piece of heavy-duty smooth plastic or similar, between 6" and 18" square (although rectangles are okay too). This will act as a printing plate, so old (smooth) floor tiles or a piece of sheet acrylic will work well (off-cuts of sheet acrylic are often available at knock-down prices). Even a small 6" ceramic tile can yield great results
- Tools to use to 'scrape' out marks in the paint; old credit cards, forks and combs, tile scrapers/grouting tools, wooden skewers, old pens (and there's always your fingers)
- A container for water
- Optional; a hard rubber roller

The Goal: to make marks and create texture by working in the negative image.

The Method
Some practice will be required in getting the layer of paint to the optimum thickness. Too thick and the print will be 'gloopy', too thin and the print will be faint. Just experiment.
1. If you're working with white paint, print on black paper/card. If you're working with black paint, print on white paper/card.
2. Using a foam brush, bristle brush or foam roller, apply a layer of paint to the 'print plate' (e.g. your piece of thick plastic, sheet acrylic etc.). Experiment until you find the optimum thickness of paint. Sometimes, the brush marks are interesting and useful in their own right.
3. Now take one of your tools and 'scratch' or etch out marks, imagery or texture into the still-wet paint. If you don't like what you've done, simply paint it out and start again. Note; the paint will need to be wet for the etching activity. If it dries out too quickly, spray it lightly with a plant mister.
4. Take the plate to your piece of paper, or take the paper to the plate; experiment with both approaches and see what works best for you.
5. Gently press the plate and the paper together; you may want to try using a hard rubber roller to achieve even contact between them.
6. Separate them and examine your print. Hang or dry flat.
7. Sometimes you can get a second print, but mono printing is usually about getting a single (mono) print.
8. Once dry, try enlarging and reducing some of your favorites.

24 | Finding Your Own Visual Language

Variations On The Theme
- Work on damp paper (think softer edges).
- Try mono printing on black or white fabric (dry or damp). It will take the paint in a different way to paper.
- Having taken your first print, lightly mist any paint left on the plate and try for a second, 'soft-edged' print, or over-print a dried print with this softer image.
- Make a first set of fine marks using something like a comb. Then make a second set of marks/images on top using a thicker scraping tool; you can often get texture and specific imagery in one go.
- Pick a subject or a shape. Mono print 10 to 20 different images based on the same topic, varying style and size as you progress.
- Try mono printing with something like rug canvas or leaves. Paint the canvas or leaf and then place paper on top to get a print.

Review
Consider:
- What was it like working in the negative image? It can seem odd at first, but it's simply a different way of seeing things. Try reversing the image to see what it looks like as a positive.
- How did any layering of etched marks work? What would happen if you made marks with 3 different tools on the same plate?
- Try over-printing dried first prints with a second print. This can give great layering effects.
- How can you adapt and experiment further with mono printing? Try using a small plate and building up several prints side-by-side on the same piece of paper, card or cloth to create an overall semi-repeat pattern.

Mono printed cloth

A selection of painted papers. These will be stacked on top of each other (Step 1)

Cutting out the first shape from the stack of papers (Step 2)

Each cut-out has been placed in a new 'home', and taped from the back to hold it in place (Steps 3 to 5)

This example shows that a second cut-out has been made and reassembled, and the third cut - clear across the papers - is under way (Steps 6 & 7)

Visual Exercise 13
Colour &
Pattern Collage

Supplies
- A collection of coloured papers (notebook size or larger), painted papers or something in your chosen colour scheme, which might be fairly monochromatic or achromatic – grey, white and black. Ideally, the papers should be thin enough to cut through 4-5 layers in one go using a craft knife. If you have thicker papers, you can use scissors instead of a knife. These papers could be elements that fit into a theme or series you're interested in and might include:
  - photocopies of fabric
  - newsprint, especially if you have an interest in the media, printing or lettering
  - wrapping papers with a variety of textures or surface patterns
  - your own painted papers with a more personal or subtle surface
  - photocopying coloured papers to change them into a b/w format is a great idea if you are interested in studying value combinations
- Tape (masking or decorators tape will do)
- A craft knife
- Scissors
- Cutting mat

The Goal: to explore value, colour and textural arrangements within a composition, using a random selection of elements within a structured collage format.

The Method
1. Stack 4-5 layers of same-size paper on top of a cutting mat. If they are light-weight enough to cut through all of the layers in one go, then consider taping the stack down at the 4 corners.
2. Cut a shape from all 4-5 layers using a craft knife. If the stack is too thick to cut through all of the layers at once, cut out a shape from the first piece of paper and use that as a template to draw the cut-out shape on to the other sheets. Then cut each sheet one-by-one. You should end up with 4 to 5 pieces of paper with the same shape cut out of them, in the same place.
3. Separate the pieces and spread them out as individual sheets in front of you.
4. Begin exchanging cut-out shapes with each other. Place one cut-out in the void left by a cut-out equivalent to it on another paper. Play with interchanging the cut-out pieces until you have a variety of compositions. Nothing should end up where it came from.
5. Stick these new 'originals' together using masking tape on the back of the pieces.
6. Repeat steps 1 to 5, varying the shape you cut out, and the place it's cut from.

The paper stack, cut right through

The final collages

7. Having cut shapes out at least twice, re-stack the pieces and this time, cut clear across them with a craft knife, scissors or a rotary cutter.
8. Separate the two sets and start playing with re-assembly options; each half should have a new partner.
9. Once you're happy (and not all of them will please you), tape them together on the back with masking tape.
10. Now re-stack them and cut clear across the stack in a new orientation.
11. Separate the two sets and once again, re-assemble them with a new partner.
12. Tape each piece of halves together from the back using masking tape.
13. At this point, you're likely to have at least two 'compositions' which have some potential. If this is the case, take them out of the stack and set them to one side.
14. Take the remaining pieces and continue cutting shapes or cutting clear across. Re-assemble the elements with different partners until one more piece has potential. You're allowed to discard any frogs on the basis that you may have found some princes.
15. If nothing pleases, start over.

Variations And Additions To The Theme
- When assembling the paper stacks, think contrasts; plain, patterned, textured, geometric, organic, matte, smooth, shiny, dull etc.
- When cutting the paper stacks think contrast; make one shape large, the next small. Make one shape geometric, the next organic. Cut a line, then a shape. Cut straight edges, cut curvy edges and so forth.
- Alter the sequence of your cutting; whilst the exercise says start by cutting shapes and then go to cutting clear across the paper, you could start the other way around, or alternate cut-out shapes with clear-across cutting.

- From time to time, re-orientate the papers when re-stacking them e.g. turn one or several pieces in the stack so what was the top becomes the bottom. If you work with a square rather than a rectangular format, you can rotate four times.
- If the collages are in colour, what will they look like in black & white (photocopy them).
- Draw or mark make into them to give a stitched effect or to add texture.
- Re-colour the black and white copies to try alternative colour ways.
- Cut them up and reassemble them again.
- Reduce them and tile them.
- Trace the individual elements within the collage to get a line study.
- If the design takes the form of a background, glue down new elements, draw or paint on it.

Review
Spend time writing about the process and the results. Let the collages talk to you and suggest ways forward, ask some questions about them and note down your answers, for example:
- How might one or several be translated into a composition (a pieced or painted textile, a painting, etc).
- Are some of the elements visually jarring? How can you change them to eliminate the discordant note?
- Has the exercise been interesting but not produced useable results? If so, why might this be and what would you do differently next time.
- How well do the collages speak to you?
- Are they useful in terms of the way you work?
- Do the collages suggest their own interpretation, or remind you of something? If so, what is it?
- What would you name each collage?
- What would you do if you were to start over?
- What could you do to adapt this technique to suit your style or topic?

Finding Your Own Visual Language | 27

Abstractions of a fork

Ruth reviews several abstract designs

Visual Exercise 14
Abstraction of an Object

Supplies
- White paper
- Black paper
- Scissors or craft knife
- Glue stick or bottled glue
- A selection of tools/objects (fork, hammer, scissors, nutcracker, cheese grater, paintbrush etc.)

Optional:
- Pens and markers

The Goal: to explore the possibilities of altering an image to make it less predictable as a design element.

The Method

Perspective is an example of visual convention. To distort perception makes a statement about reality. When Cubists distorted reality they were encouraging the viewer to think differently about the world around them. This is one point of abstraction – to surprise the viewer enough to allow reconsideration of the nature of reality.

- Choose a tool and draw a factual silhouette of it. For example – draw around the hammer, or draw the pair of scissors as they appear flat on the paper.
- Now draw four different sizes of shaped 'boxes' on the white paper. For example, one box may be a square, one a rectangle, one a triangle etc. Make the boxes different sizes but don't make any of them exceptionally small. The cut outs or drawings you will be creating need to fit inside the boxes you've drawn.
- It might help to think of the tool as rubber. If you have a triangular box to fill, how could you squeeze or stretch or bend the fork so that it will fit inside the box?
- Consider changing proportions. The tool does not need to look or be functional. It is important to keep the essence of the tool. For a fork, that might be the tines. For a hammer it would probably be the recognizable claw and head. How far can you push or bend or stretch or change the tool while keeping the essence that is recognizable?
- Draw or cut out only the essential lines that make up the object. The object should FILL UP the box you're currently addressing.
- Re-configure the tool four times so that it will fit inside the different boxes you drew.
- Do 6 to 8 - examples are important in this exercise.

Variations And Additions To The Theme
- Try using the 'What if?' commands in Exercise 15: what if you make the fork funny or silly? What if you stretch it or shrink it?
- Try applying moods, adjectives or adverbs to your chosen implement. We made the fork feel 'wilted' or 'depressed'. We turned it into a tree and we made it dance. We turned it into a candleabra by fitting it into a landscape rectangle and exploded it out by fitting it into a circle. Sometimes, using words rather than drawn boxes will help you to abstract your chosen object.
- Use fruit or vegetables instead of tools… or even people or animals. What characteristics must something have in order to make an interesting abstracted image? Is it quantifiable?
- Use pen or marker to draw an abstracted version of the tool or subject.
- Trace the abstracted images you made – along the line of Visual Exercise No. 3.
- Expand or reduce the images on the photocopier to alter them even more significantly.

Review
Consider:
- How recognizable are your abstractions? It doesn't matter hugely if they're not, as many interesting shapes can come out of the exercise. Equally, have you captured the 'essence' of the thing?
- Learning to abstract objects, ideas and concepts is one of the most valuable skills you can acquire. The more you practice the better you get at doing it.

The holly leaf waiting to be abstracted

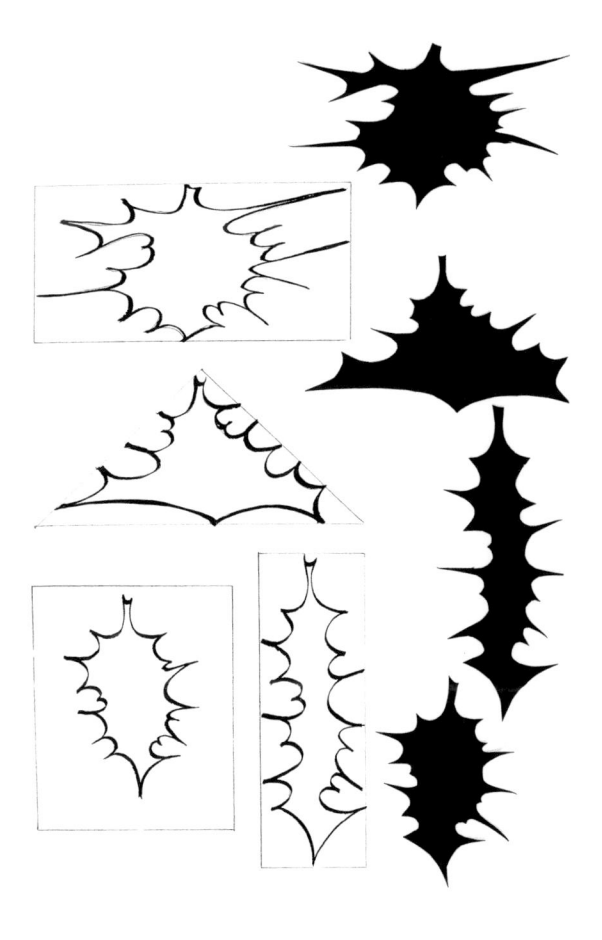

Abstracted holly leaves: the original leaf shape is at bottom right, with its outline tracing bottom left

Finding Your Own Visual Language | 29

Visual Exercise 15
What If?

A grid, drawn with an italic felt-tip pen

What if I...distort or twist the grid?

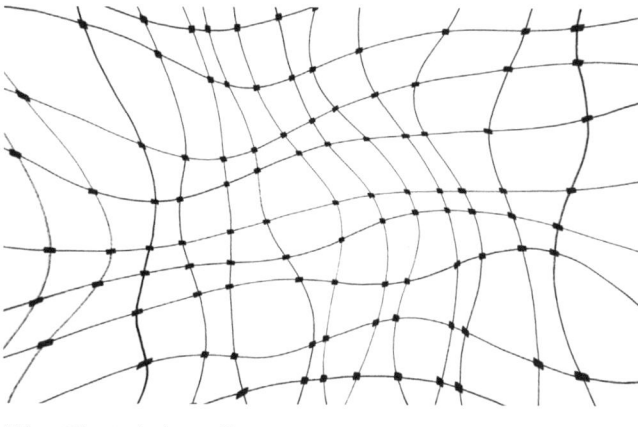

What if I...pinch the grid?

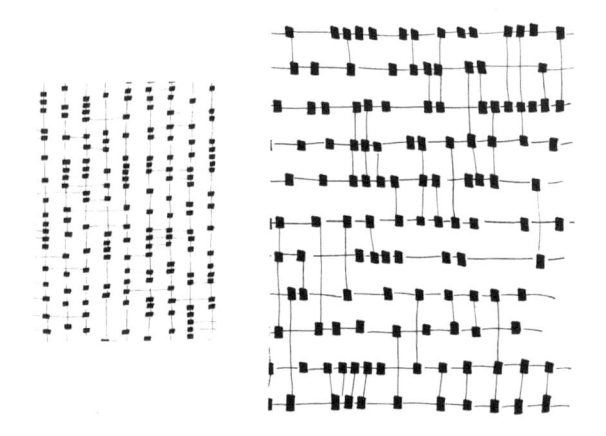

What if I...make the grid smaller?

Supplies
- Notebook and pencil for brainstorming 'what if' ideas
- A computer; if you're confident at using the computer to manipulate images, it will speed things up for this exercise
- Otherwise, re-create the image in a different way using the materials you used for the original exercise

The Goal: sometimes you need a prompt to get the creative brain going. Using "what if" commands can help.

The Method
1. Use any of your images/designs - originals or enlarged/reduced versions - whichever appeals to you.
2. Choose a "what if" and apply it to the image. Play about.
3. Try several different terms with the same image.

What if I make it...						
Bigger	Smaller	Tiny	Round	Short	Tall/Long	Fatter
Thin	Square	Into a set	Stronger	Cooler	Hotter	Fly
Heavy	Light	Transparent	Bend	Symmetrical	Wonky	Lay flat
Fragile	Opaque	Funny	Silly	Childish	Romantic	Satirical
Ancient	Modern	Nostalgic	Futuristic	Balanced	Weird	Scary

What if I...			
Fill it up	Empty it	Lay it down	Coil it
Open it up	Turn it upside down	Stretch it	Shrink it
Eliminate bits of it	Change it to a shape	Give it texture	Reverse it
Bend it	Swirl it	Fatten it	Enlarge it

Variations And Additions To The Theme
- Using the "what if" principal, come up with your own words and then apply them.
- Select three of the terms and actually alter an image based on the words you've selected.

Review
Consider:
- Working with the terms offers an opportunity to explore stylistic differences in your approach to representing an image. Ancient versus modern interpretation, for example, is a study in style as much as it is a study of any other quality.
- Working with terms also encourages you to explore the abstraction of your imagery. Read the Abstraction of an Object Exercise on page 28 to get a better understanding of abstraction and it's potential.
- Be on the look out for potential imagery drawn from the words we've suggested. A word may be a key to a whole new line of thinking and creation.

Visual Exercise 16
What's Emerging?

Supplies
- Notebook
- Pen or pencil

The Goal: sometimes, all of this drawing, cutting, glueing etc. can allow your subconscious to speak, leading to the discovery of a theme, story or message within your visual exercises (and this is true of any written exercises you may have done or eventually do.)

The Method
1. Take some time out. Go back and look at what you've produced. Pay attention.
2. Are similar marks, images or motifs appearing? If so, start "bundling" them together in groups (as there may be more than one theme to be found)
3. Look at these bundled images… can you sense a theme, story or message, a body of work? If so, what is it?
4. If you didn't have a theme to begin with, or a subject for a body of work, but find it through this review, it's time to:
   - Focus in on it.
   - Undertake more visual exercises around it.
   - Free associate with it (see the exercises in the Going Deeper chapter).

Variations On The Theme
- If you did have a theme before you began these exercises, how pleased are you with the imagery you've developed?
- What else could you do to develop the existing imagery further?
- What other exercises (visual or written) might be considered to develop your theme?

Review
Consider:
- There are as many ways to discover thematic material as there are people working to do so. Stay open.
- Don't undervalue the power of the unconscious to work when you think you're not working. Sleep, rest, exercise, dance – all valid ways of encouraging the mind to work on it's own for a while.

In Conclusion

Completing these exercises – no matter how many of them you finish – will be enormously helpful. Only you can decide what tools they'll become, or how you'll use what you create in quilts, stitched textiles, art cloth, embroidery or whatever your chosen discipline is. But the foundation will be laid for the work that comes next…the mastery of the language you'll need to analyze and discuss the work you create.

Let's take a look at that next.

Contrasts of scale and shape in the imagery (Jeanne Beck, 'Source')

Moving Forward

Let's talk about qualities that contribute interest, intrigue, and power to visual surfaces. Studying and understanding the language of design is part of learning to add interest, intrigue and visual power to your own work.

A design lexicon does exist – it's the language of art schools and textbooks. However, we believe basic design principles can be described in simpler terms. This isn't an idea we developed on our own. Like all good ideas inspired by other good ideas, the design language we use was inspired by a great book called *'Picture This: How Pictures Work'*, by Molly Bang. Her book is straightforward, simply written and it observes the following:

- Design principles are rooted in human reaction to the world around us. We feel safe when we're lying down – so flat surfaces and straight lines feel safe, for example.
- Vertical lines are uplifting in a design because they lift our eyes to the Heavens.
- Diagonal lines guide our eyes and add interest to a design.
- Sharp points and angles trigger anxiety – which isn't always obvious because it is subliminal – the human brain automatically relates sharp points to knives, spears and other objects that can hurt physically.
- Smooth, rolling images remind us of our mother's bodies. The psychic reaction is to relax and feel calmed.

Molly's book is a delightful, easily understood guide to basic design principals, and we recommend it. Her approach inspired our approach – to discuss design elements in the context of human psychology and emotion. We won't use words like *unity*, or *continuation* - but not because they aren't perfectly good terms. It's just that other words are often easier for people to GET. Our goal is to translate design terminology into a contemporary, easily utilized language.

Principles versus Tools

Which leads to this important distinction: **Principles** are fundamental design ideas rooted in the physical world. Human beings have absolutely no control over them, just as we can't control the physical response of our eyes to bright light. The basic principles are always true. An experienced artist learns how to work with design principles to shape the viewer's experience of his or her work.

When we discuss **Tools** in this particular design conversation, we don't mean stamps, brushes, or a needle and thread. Design Tools are the devices artists manipulate in order to maximize their use of the Principles. Tools are used to organize compositions so the Principles will have maximum effect. Which means we DO have control over how we combine and use design tools in order to achieve specific visual results.

So – what should you know about organizing space, in order to manage it effectively? We've focused on five key elements: Contrast & Relationship, Focal Point, Balance and Integration.

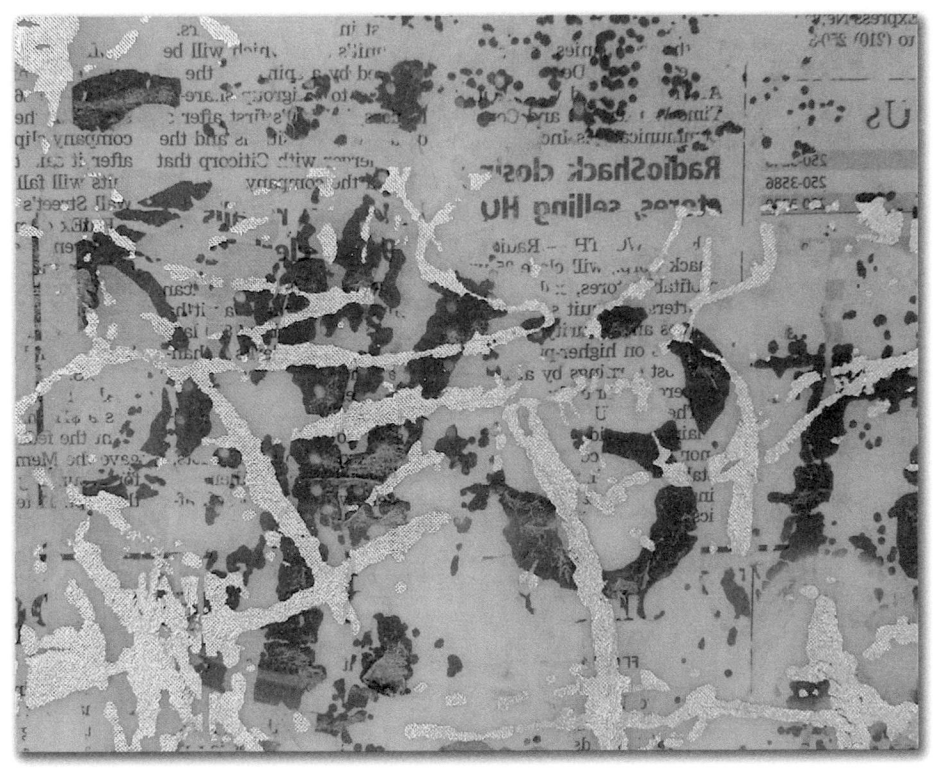

Detail of 'Babylon'
Jane Dunnewold

*A complementary colour scheme
(detail, Claire Benn)*

An analogous colour scheme with added sparkle (detail, Jane Dunnewold)

Contrast of texture (Jane Dunnewold, 'Choir' detail)

Contrast & Relationship

Contrasts and relationships are basic principles, and a good place to start. Contrast is key to generating interest. Without contrast, we have nothing to consider. There are a number of tools we use to generate **Contrast** on a surface and they include:

- **Color;** a range of color combinations is at our fingertips. For example, complementary, analogous and triadic schemes.

- **Value;** contrasting light, medium and darker values provide a sense of implied depth.

- **Size:** small, medium and large scale images and design elements. Useful to note that size is extremely subjective, and also relative to the other elements included in the composition, and the size of the overall piece.

- **Shape:** as simple as squares combined with triangles or circles, or as sophisticated as solid forms contrasted with linear or more delicately patterned shapes.

- **Texture;** one of the most useful ways to generate contrast. Texture can be REAL – matte paint printed on a shiny charmeuse fabric or shiny foil laminated to a piece of cloth - or IMPLIED: texture printed using a variety of tools and designed to add contrast to specific areas of the fabric surface, while not actually a textural contrast that can be touched and felt.

- **Stylistic Contrast;** the use of varying styles – sometimes of the same element (alphabets or letters for example) and sometimes of similar elements (art deco fans contrasted with Asian styling or contemporary elements).

- **Thematic Contrast;** within a particular story line, there may be a variety of images combined, each of which plays a role in supporting the overall theme. For example, let's say we've devised a "garden" theme – flowers, seed packets, line drawings of the garden's outline, color selection. All are elements that relate to the theme, but each is different from the other – hence providing the contrast.

Elements of contrast exist on a continuum. At one end is the subtle - what might be described as "Asian" aesthetic – simple patterning, simple color schemes: perhaps a monochromatic one relying on value to provide contrast. This is "quiet" visual work. The other end of the continuum represents high contrast, busy, visual surfaces. Contrasts of all kinds are effective. A range of variations exist when selecting and applying contrast to any surface.

This piece shows a strong thematic image, good value contrast and relationships (Maggie Weiss, 'Goddess' series)

Finding Your Own Visual Language | 35

Contrasts of scale, colour, value and texture, coupled with diverse imagery (artcloth detail, Jane Dunnewold)

The piece on the left is monochromatic, the piece on the right demonstrates good color and value contrast (work-in-progress, Linda Maynard)

Contrast of texture (real and implied), value and line (Christina Ellcock, detail of work-in-progress)

Strong thematic elements at work, with contrasts of colour, value, size and texture (Bente Volde Klausen, 'Mother of the Earth')

Relationship is another important principle of successful visual surfaces. Choosing to build relationship means the maker has deliberately selected design elements and colors to create a well-integrated surface. It's a wonderfully delicious irony that the same tools used to generate contrast serve to build relationship.

Consider:

- **Color;** the same range of color relationships is available as when we were generating contrast. How we choose to use or combine colors affects whether the piece feels disjointed or integrated. A monochromatic theme is subdued and calmer than a complementary theme, and a bright dose of complement against a background color "pops" visually.

- **Size;** ordering size builds relationship (small, medium and large), as does using two different elements of the same size.

- **Shape;** curvy elements may be distinct from each other but share qualities of shape, which contribute to the sense of relationship.

- **Value:** a smooth transition between light, medium and dark elements contributes a sense of movement to the surface and also enhances the implied sense of depth.

- **Texture:** whilst used more frequently for contrast, texture is particularly useful in an abstract composition when relationships can't rely on specific imagery to integrate the surface.

- **Stylistic Relationship;** it's easier to build relationship in a composition if the design elements are stylistically alike. It is more difficult to combine elements if they are dissimilar stylistically because they may feel out of sync. For example, if you've hand-drawn images of leaves and flowers in a composition and then introduce a Victorian image or a contemporary, photo-realistic image, the visual flow between the images may be broken because the style of the image is too different from those that preceded it.

- **Thematic Relationship;** it's hard to produce a cohesive composition if thought isn't given to the relationship between the design elements you plan to combine. Throwing any available image at the surface is a common beginner's error, because you're short on tools and impatient to get on with it. Strong work requires thought go into the combination of images so they work together effectively to tell the story.

Finding Your Own Visual Language | 37

We enter the piece and the leaves take the eye up, around and down again.
(Leslie Morgan, Dangerous Journey-Standing Still, detail)

This piece glows and the gold marks provide subtle secondary accents and visual bridges (Els van Baarle, 'Spine')

The gold rings provide secondary accents to the strong door into this piece (Jane Dunnewold, 'Boundary Waters')

Focal Point - The Door Into The Picture World

We said we weren't going to use terms like focal point as part of our quest for simple terminology, but it's a term we must mention as part of reshaping concepts.

Instead of describing it as the focal point, call it the *door into the picture world*. And remember, the picture world is the composition. If you paint canvas, the picture world is the canvas. If you quilt, the picture world is the quilt. If you work on lengths of cloth, the entire length is the picture world. If you embroider, your embroidery is the picture world. You get the idea. The door into the picture world is the TOOL an artist uses to attract the viewer's interest when he or she looks at a composition. The door into the picture world is almost always a result of contrast: color, size, shape, texture, or value. Stylistic and thematic contrasts are "overall" issues and aren't key to entry into the composition.

One common misconception is that a composition or picture world has only one entry point. It is certainly true that one element can grab your eyes when you look at piece of artwork and then convince you to take a look around. But it is also possible, and just as legitimate, to include more than one entry point.

It works like this – your eyes go to one high contrast element - that's the door or entry to get you inside the composition. Next you notice a series of other elements, which lead your eyes around or across the surface. They play an important role when it comes to keeping you looking, but they are secondary elements since none of them were the initial reason you started looking at the 'picture'. In many compositions - including lengths of cloth or yardage - there are several elements leading the viewer's eye across the surface, or around inside the picture world. When a picture is built using this format we refer to those elements as the *secondary accents*.

It's also true that a picture world or composition may not have an entry point at all. Color field painting and traditional pieced quilts are examples of a style that doesn't include elements designed to grab your attention first or move the eye. The thing to remember is the importance of INTENT. When an entry point or door into the composition is lacking, it is usually because leaving it out was intentional. So the lack of an obvious, contrasting element was deliberate, and that's part of the artist's message.

A high horizon line (Ingrid Press, 'Tulips')

Finding Your Own Visual Language | 39

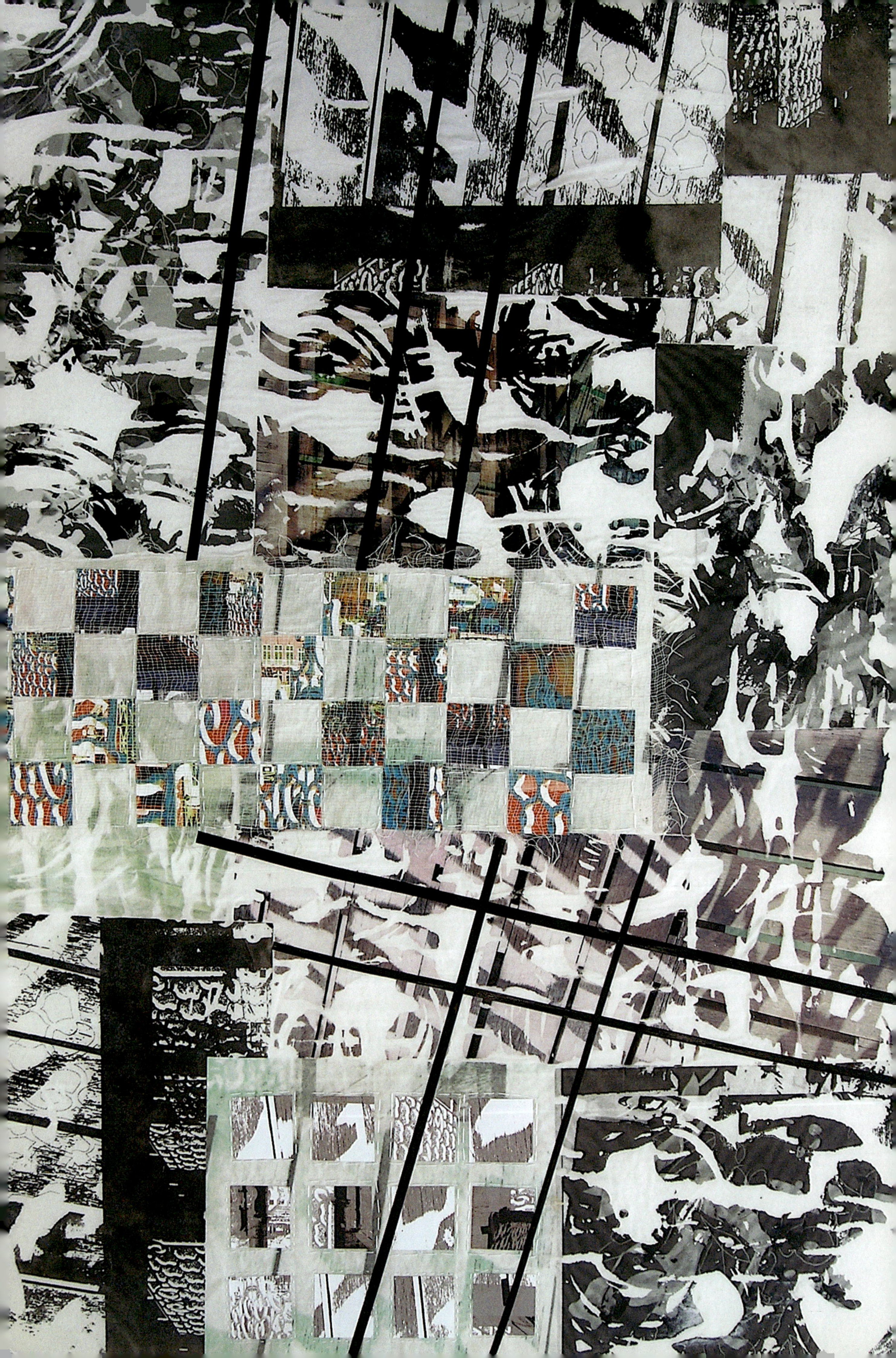

Strong symmetrical balance
(Cheryl Collins, detail, work-in-progress)

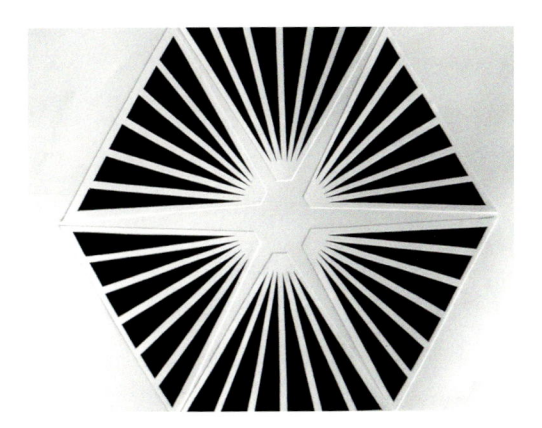

Radial balance

Crystallographic balance
(Christina Ellcock, detail, work-in-progress)

Balance
Balance is a Principle generated through thoughtful use of the design tools. There are four basic forms of balancing a composition. (Remember, the composition is the picture world.)

Symmetrical Balance
Simply put, a mirror image. Good example? Any classical building in which the right and left sides (as you stand looking at the building) are identical. Symmetrical balance is used to generate a solid, safe, simple and trustworthy composition. If we look at nineteenth century bank buildings and churches, we'll discover they are architecturally symmetrical buildings. The underlying psychological message is "your money (or your faith) is safe with us". Symmetry is not used very often in contemporary artwork, but when it is, the picture world feels solid and stable. Symmetrical balance can be achieved through placement of identical elements side by side OR by the placement of identical elements in the top and bottom halves of a composition.

Asymmetrical Balance
Balance of this type is achieved through placement of the design elements – whether abstract OR representational ones. Asymmetrical balance is never exactly the same. The achievement of it varies according to how the tools of contrast and relationship are used. Sometimes placement of elements helps lead the eye across the composition in addition to providing balance. Sometimes one element is the door or entry into the composition, and is also an element contributing to balance. Remember; tools don't exist in a vacuum and various design elements often play more than one role in a composition.

Radial Balance
The words provide the clue. Radial balance is a series of elements that radiate out from the center of the picture. The (originally Hindu or Buddhist) Mandala is a classic example of radial balance. Mandalas were usually circular and used to express the universe or a person's striving for unity of the self. Because this balance is achieved by centering the important design elements, the viewer's eye returns to the center of the composition again and again. This form of balance is selected when the goal is "centering". It is a format of many spiritual traditions where it is deliberately used to direct attention to a message conveyed by the imagery. When a contemporary artist uses radial balance, it is usually because the quality of returning again and again to the center of the composition is an important aspect of Intent.

Crystallographic Balance
This is an all-over approach to the organization of the composition. Traditional quilt blocks assembled into a repeating pattern are one example of crystallographic balance. Any all-over pattern – whether in a painting, or a length of fabric - employs this approach to composition. Another way to think about crystallographic balance is this - the composition may be interesting and elements may lead the eye, but a single door into the picture world is not apparent.

There is tremendous value in becoming comfortable with these basic terms. If you know the language it is easier to share a conversation with other artists as part of a critique, but it can also aid private analysis of work in progress. Just remember that design tools don't usually perform alone. They are almost always in concert with other tools, playing a variety of roles to support the basic principles. And tools aren't purists. Slight shifts away from the purest version of usage are common, and welcome. The primary goal is to achieve balance, intriguing contrast, and a sense of relationship, while striving for Integration and Elegance.

Left: Asymmetry at work (Christina Ellcock, work-in-progress)

Contrasts of colour, value, texture, size and shape. Well integrated and balanced with a strong door into the picture world (Charlotte Yde, 'Souvenir' series, detail)

*Contrasts of colour, value, texture, size and shape. The blue circles provide a pathway through the piece and red squares support the upward lift
(Claire Benn, 'Square Pegs, Round Holes')*

Integration & Visual Bridges – More Simple Terms

There are a few more ideas worth adding to a discussion of design principles and tools.

Integration

One principle, which could also be described as a goal, is Integration. When a picture is integrated it exhibits the three key qualities of Balance, Relationship and Contrast. Let's quickly re-visit these with an eye for Integration:

Balance; remember the four forms of Balance covered in the previous section: Symmetrical, Asymmetrical, Radial and Crystallographic. No matter which form has been chosen, balance exists and no individual parts feel as if they're going to topple the picture or fall out of the composition. No element is too big or too small. The parts "fit" and work together cohesively.

Relationship: the second aspect of integration is the Relationship among or between individual design elements. If there is a style, the elements support it. If there is a theme, the elements contribute to it. Every element is important and no element could be removed without weakening the overall impact or structure of the picture/composition. No element is discordant or jarring.

Contrast: the third aspect of integration is the effective use of Contrast. We noted the list of tools used to generate contrast. It is important to recognize that if individual elements exhibit too much contrast the whole piece may suffer from a lack of integration. The parts are so disparate they don't hang together.

So, you can see the two extremes of the continuum when it comes to the use of contrast and relationship. If relationships are weak or not well planned, or contrast is too disconnected and doesn't make sense, then the work will suffer from a lack of integration. And if the work doesn't exhibit contrast, doesn't have a door into the picture world, or relationships are too predictable and mundane, it will suffer because it can't hold the viewer's interest. It's boring. Neither thing is a good thing.

Integration is achieved through balance, contrast & relationship (Jane Dunnewold, 'Balancing Act', detail)

Finding Your Own Visual Language | 43

Visual Bridges

The Visual Bridge is a design principle used to solve contrast problems. The visual bridge is a *Principle* - it can be applied to any of the seven tools used to generate contrast or build relationship. For example, a design may feel out of balance because tiny elements are paired with overly large elements. The visual bridge is the addition of a medium sized design motif. The medium sized element bridges the visual gap between the small and large motifs.

Sometimes the needed *visual bridge* is a color bridge. It visually connects two colors that are not related by adding a third color that relates to each of the other two. For example, if a composition combines bright green and red it can be visually jarring. A color bridge – a mixture of the two, generating rust or olive or brown – softens the contrast by pulling the red and green closer together visually.

Visual bridges are always elements that refine *Integration* of a composition by building relationship. One question you can ask when a composition isn't working is this one – would the surface benefit from the addition of a visual bridge?

The Elegant Choice

When you make art you are faced with numerous choices. Every time you add a new shape, color, or texture, every time you play with balance, or placement of the *door into the picture world*, you have several choices. More than one of them probably "works" in the overall scheme of the composition.

But there is usually one best choice over the others. Think of it as the *perfect choice*. No other color, placement, size, or shape would be better than the one you've chosen. This is referred to as an Elegant Choice. Perhaps more an ideal than a reality, the elegant choice implies an immersion in the decision making process. You are centered. You are thoughtful. You don't flail or settle. Patience is also implied, as these decisions don't happen immediately most of the time, although they can be propelled by a sudden burst of intuition. Striving for the elegant choice is worth it because it is a very satisfying approach to the act of making. The delight in your *product* is balanced by the delight in your *process*.

So, to summarise we'd say that having generated visual imagery to use in your work, the challenge is to use it effectively. Understanding and practicing the principles and tools of design lays a firm foundation for experimentation and exploration. Before you know it, your quest for the elegant choice is underway. Perfection is out there and doing the work is your surest shot at achieving it.

And once you're doing the work, ask yourself this question now and again: How's it Going?

A real sense of looking through is provided by the graphic black lines against the paler, textural background. The piece is beautifully balanced by the placement of the red. The eye is encouraged to explore through the vertical. Elegant choices have been made to achieve a well-integrated piece
Christina Ellcock, 'Paper Fruit'

Value contrasts provide balance. The bright, white leaves float on the surface whilst shape, line and texture encourage us to explore deeper into the piece
Leslie Morgan, 'Lost Light'

Finding Your Own Visual Language

How's it Going?

Okay. You've got some good ideas. The quilt design is set. The sketch of the embroidery has been fleshed out with colour ideas. The imagery is waiting to be expressed in your chosen medium. It's time to create the work. In the introduction we mentioned that mastering technique is important if the work is to be strong. So identify the best method of translating your designs and imagery then practice, practice, practice.

This isn't a book about mastering technique. We can only assume you'll work toward mastery, utilising whatever resources and help you have available. On that basis we've also assumed that you'll get to a point where you'll stand back, take a look and ask yourself "how's it going?".

There are times when you work and the piece flows from your hands like water. The initial effort you put in pays dividends and things are shaping up just as you intended. The question of "how's it going?" is never an issue until it's not going well.

However, sooner or later you'll hang a piece up, step back and realise that something's not right. The realisation that it's not going well is always uncomfortable. It's easy to focus wholly on the problem, rather than solution. The first step is to try to reframe the problem and put it in balance. Einstein said "in the middle of difficulty lies opportunity". So, take a deep breath and…

Take Time for Contemplation & Evaluation

Identifying the specific cause of the problem – and the corresponding solutions – is going to take time, so set time aside. Remind yourself it's an important and vital part of the overall process. To begin with, get yourself – and the work – in a positive place:

- If appropriate, start by pressing or ironing textile pieces. Hanging up a crumpled piece of cloth doesn't give it a fair chance. Neither does it respect the time and effort you've put in so far. Likewise with a pieced quilt top; get rid of loose threads. Tidy things up in order to give the work a decent start.
- Pin the piece up on a board, tape it to a wall, place it on an easel/stand. Don't try to contemplate and evaluate work flat on the table or the bench. Perspective is good.
- Set aside the victim or the persecutor in your head. By all means acknowledge their existence but refuse to engage with them on a negative level. Claim the grown-up, the adult, the rational self.
- Keep the 'critique' impersonal and objective – adopt an attitude of curiosity rather than judgment.
- Begin by asking very specific questions based on the compositional aspects (see the checklist).
- Think about what you're saying to yourself. Try to be constructive with what you have to say and be kind in the way you say it.
- Take notes of your responses and ideas.

Using The Principles & Tools Of Composition As A Checklist

We recommend you start your evaluation by working your way through the following questions based around the principles and tools of composition;

Integration/Composition

- Does everything 'fit' or belong?
- Are there good relationships between the different elements? Or would a visual bridge help (e.g. size, shape, color etc.)?
- Is the piece balanced? Or does the composition feel lopsided or heavy?
- Is the 'door into the picture world' (composition) working as you intended? Does it need strengthening or is it too dominant/obvious?
- Is there an unintentional bull's eye?
- Is an element leading your eye out of the picture?
- Does any element need to be repositioned to be better balanced?
- Does any element feel too big? Or too small?
- If the color of an element were to be changed, would the balance be better?

Karen discusses two works-in-progress

The paper collage used as the source for the palette of cloth

Contrast
Is there…
- size contrast?
- colour contrast?
- value contrast?
- shape contrast?
- textural contrast?
- stylistic contrast?
- thematic contrast?
- Where could additional contrast strengthen the piece visually?

Relationship
- Is there a clear sense of colour relationship(s)?
- Do value relationships exist or make sense?
- Are there coherent size relationships?
- Are there coherent shape relationships?
- Are there useful textural relationships?
- Do the stylistic relationships make sense?
- Are thematic relationships supported by the combination of design and colour elements?
- Where could the sense of relationship among the various parts be strengthened?

Colour
- Does any colour strike you immediately as being "off"?
- Can colour use be supported by theory? (Even if it is in the simple terms of a basic colour wheel). Do colours feel connected? Or would a visual bridge help unify the surface?
- Would adding a brighter colour make the composition more interesting? Or does a colour need toning or calming down?
- Would removing any colour make the composition stronger?
- Would a high contrast colour element add focus to help move the eye?

And finally, consider evaluating workmanship; finishing, straight edges (if appropriate), presentation and so forth.

As you answer these questions, acknowledge the good aspects of the work. This will help you stay in balance and motivated. These simple "yes" and "no" questions are designed to identify specific issues leading to solutions. You've started 'funneling', moving from the broad to the specific. Next, dig deeper to encourage specific ideas to flow.

The 'palette' of cloth created from the collage (Leslie Morgan)

46 | Finding Your Own Visual Language

Seeking Solutions & Making Decisions

Funneling from the broad to the specific involves focusing and asking more questions. Use 'open' questions that can't be answered by "yes" or "no". The key ones to use begin with *what, how, where and which*. The answers to the questions provide information, which can then drive solutions. For example, let's say you've narrowed it down to issues around contrast in value. The conversation with yourself might go like this:

Q; *There isn't enough range from light to dark, so what could be done about that?*
A; I have a choice between adding darker elements, lighter elements or perhaps both.
Q; *Okay, what impact would adding darker tones have, and what impact would adding lighter tones have? And what would happen if both were added simultaneously?*
A; I'll opt to add darker elements.
Q; *Of the elements that make up the piece – such as the shapes or the texture – which would be best used to manipulate the value contrast?*
A; I think I'll use the shapes.
Q; *Great, so what size would work best and what placement makes sense?*

Let's now consider another example of how things can go askew: the possibility that your piece isn't achieving the original intention – it's not moving toward the idea you had in your head. Once again, the answers lie in the questions.

Observation; it's not meeting my original intent, it's not up to the vision inside my head.
Question; *so what – specifically - do I feel is wrong here? How am I failing to meet the needs of my vision?"*
Observation; it's a bit linear, and I didn't want that.
Question; *… linear in what way?*
Observation; I've got a lot of pretty straight horizontals and those rigid rows don't convey the sense of crowd I wanted.
Question; *how can I get a better sense of crowd and how big a crowd do I want - how many people constitute a crowd?*
Observation; more than I've got, that's for sure – what I'm seeing is more of a raggle-taggle, spread out bunch of people – there aren't enough and they're all in rows.
Question; *so what's the opposite of putting things in rows – what have I got to do differently?*
Observation; I need to work in a more organic way using random, jumbled-up placement – and I need a lot more than I've got there already.
Observation/Decision; So I'll try that….

Talk to yourself and with the piece from a standpoint of curiosity rather than judgment or despair. Being judgemental will drive negativity and undermine your confidence. Negativity drives despair, hopelessness and self-pity. Shake yourself out of this and try to re-frame things. Remember Einstein: "in the middle of difficulty lies opportunity". Seek objectivity, acceptance and a forward strategy. A forward strategy means acknowledging mistakes, learning from them and coming up with ways to correct or improve the situation.

If asking questions/having a conversation with the piece doesn't produce answers or solutions, try asking one big question, e.g. "I need to beef up the contrast in terms of value – how can I do that?". Write down every single idea that comes into your head. Consider setting a time limit for this activity and don't stop to evaluate each idea, just list as many as you can.

Jane and Linda contemplate work-in-progress

Claire Higgott comtemplates the progress of 'Shooting the Past'

Finding Your Own Visual Language | 47

Move on to consider each idea as objectively as possible:

- the advantages and disadvantages
- how will it move the piece forward
- what purpose will it serve

Remember, the most elegant solution aspires to be the most perfect solution. No other colour, placement, shape or size would be better than the one you've chosen. Immerse yourself in this decision-making process. Be thoughtful. Try not to flail about and don't settle for 'that'll do'. Be patient and accept that contemplation and decision-making take time and are valuable processes.

Engage with your ideas before committing to them – whilst there are no guarantees, there are ways of 'auditioning', for example;

- draw, print or photocopy the element(s) you're considering on acetates/transparencies. Audition different placements or combinations of placements on the piece using these acetates.
- use painted paper, sheers, scraps of cloth, coloured sheets of acetate or even magazine cuttings in the same way.
- cut out the shape(s) you want to use in different sizes. Use card, paper (coloured or black and white), painted paper, newspaper or photocopies of your original imagery.
- use threads of different weights to mimic additional texture or potential stitching/quilting lines.

And if in doubt, try it out.

Some Rules Of Thumb
Here are some other things you can do…

- **Re-orientate the work;** whilst you may have made the piece to be viewed a certain way 'up', try rotating it through 90°, four times to enable you to view it from all four orientations. Who knows, it may just want to be upside down, or landscape rather than portrait.

- **Change the scale/format of the work;** what would happen if a portion of the work were to be shaved off… the top, the bottom, the left or the right? Try folding back or masking out edges to see what happens. Sometimes a rectangular piece suddenly works more effectively when square, shortened, or made more slender. Sometimes a square piece wants to be a rectangle. Spend some time considering the scale/format.

- **Back off a little:** if ideas or decisions don't materialise as quickly as you'd like, set the piece aside, but look at it now and then. Sometimes a solution just pops into your head. Trust your intuition, otherwise you may do nothing and suffer from 'analysis paralysis'. We don't want you to settle for "that'll do" but do accept that some solutions won't work. You have to kiss a lot of frogs before you find the prince!

Everything here belongs and is as it should be. We're given a great deal to look at without things being chaotic. Integration has been achieved
Charlotte Yde, 'Bloody Garden', detail

Claire Benn, 'Pressure Point'

- **Have two or three projects on the go:** evaluating, seeking solutions and making decisions is time-consuming. To offset the frustration have two or three projects on the go. Move between them to keep your work momentum going. Remember, working on one piece can generate ideas or solutions for another.

- **Do what you believe is right for the piece:** sometimes a solution you choose may resolve the piece compositionally but move it away from your original intent. This can be a difficult thing to acknowledge as on the one hand, you want to have integrity and keep pushing to achieve your intention. On the other hand, there's a difference between intention and obsession. Be careful you don't become too attached to the original idea to the point that you put on blinders. Work can take on a life of its own and have a say about where it wants to go. Listen to the work and consider what it's got to say. A piece that's well resolved compositionally is still successful even if it doesn't match the vision you had inside your head. Do what you believe is right for the piece and learn from it. Then start using what you've learned on something new. This is the value of working in a series.

- **Look for several small compositions within the whole:** sometimes, no matter how hard you try, the work just won't resolve itself. Don't abandon it yet. Use a pair of cardboard 'L's (see page 11) to establish if there are several small, perfect compositions to be found within the whole. Whilst ending up with several small compositions may not have been your intention, it can be satisfying to create several small pieces.

- **Produce on two levels:** you're engaged in a balancing act and a journey of discovery. We appreciate that it is difficult to work not knowing the outcome. Being willing to do loads of work that may only move a single idea forward is labor intensive and requires guts. One way to cope is to produce on two levels. Work on pieces that are likely to be successful, but also make work that won't ever go anywhere but perhaps the trash – but serves your bigger picture. Eventually the two will merge. Some of your best, most innovative ideas will come from experiments. And refining your successful experiments leads to work that is uniquely your own.

- **If the horse is dead, get off it:** there's a huge amount of learning to be found in trying to resolve a composition. But - hard though it is - there may come a time when it's better to accept that something just isn't going to make it. Don't flog a dead horse. Get off it. Burn the piece, bury the piece, trash the piece, cut the piece up and use it for collage work. Extract learning from the experience and move on.

Going Deeper

At some point you may find yourself itching to engage in purposeful work. Perhaps you want to conceptualize ideas from within. For example - " I want to tackle dyslexia as a topic." Or maybe you are inspired by the physical world and you'd like to respond to this external inspiration in a tangible form – "I want to communicate the beauty of the beach in winter". Either way, you have something to communicate visually on a deeper level.

That said, it's okay if you don't want to delve deeper. Intentional work - work that achieves what you intend to express - is valuable work at any level. If you work with intent the work <u>will</u> be meaningful because of your investment in it.

We believe that the process of planning and making art triggers ideas and concepts that ultimately need to be taken further. It's important to pay attention to the work you're making. Given a chance to speak, it can suggest new ideas or angles. Don't discount the ability of your subconscious to speak through the exercises you complete. It's not unusual for themes, specific marks, and similar words to recur. Pay attention to them – they want to be seen, heard and considered. Make time to think, and to look for connections between topics and ideas that matter to you.

Offering advice on where and how to start is tricky. There are no set rules. The desire for *intention* happens to different people in different ways. For example, let's say you throw yourself into doing the visual exercises with no particular destination in mind. You review the output. Certain images resonate or trigger specific ideas/areas. You decide to focus on them. You write about the ideas and do free association exercises. Next you adapt the imagery you have and create additional images. Then do more writing, followed by thinking about colour. And so on. Back and forth, back and forth until you know what you want to say, and have a fairly clear idea about how to say it.

On the other hand, you may be ready to explore a specific idea. You could start by writing a story or a letter about it. Next do free association exercises, followed by visual imagery. Alternatively, you can begin by assembling a new collection or 'stash' box as a way of gathering things together. You could choose a single object to sketch or photograph. Maybe do some free association followed by more imagery. There's no definitive place to start. The process itself helps establish a preferred way of working. So just start digging.

The activities and reminders in this chapter are designed to encourage you to seek a deeper level of work, and we thought it would be useful to begin with a couple of case studies to put the process into context.

It all began with 'Dunce' (see Case Study 1: 'It's all Academic')
Claire Benn

Case Study 1 - 'It's all Academic' Claire Benn

It began with a mistake. I'd been asked to make something for my stepson. As a dyslexic, I knew he'd be amused by something with lettering so I began to print an alphabet. I made a mistake, printing the same letter twice. My first reaction was one of dismay, followed by the recognition that written mistakes are commonplace for a dyslexic. I went on to make deliberate mistakes and the piece resolved itself. It wasn't what I'd planned originally, but when Fate steps in, what can you do?

Whilst working, I chewed over dyslexia as a topic and decided to develop a small series. I like to begin with writing, as I generally find it generates lots of clues, fast. I began with 4 headings and did a loose free association around each one -

- 100 lines; a punishment for any kind of school discretion. Typically, what might be set as those 100 lines?
- Feelings as a dyslexic - if I was dyslexic, how might I feel?
- Comments from teachers - what might a frustrated teacher say to a dyslexic?
- School reports - what might be written in a school report about a dyslexic?

30 minutes into this exercise I realized I didn't have to imagine all of this (although it had helped). The answers were readily available in AJ's school reports, giving me the perfect research data. I dug them out and settled down to read. What emerged was a jumbled bunch of positive and negative commentary. The over-riding impression of the reports? Here was a slacker, a ne're-do-well. I wanted to get a better grip on what had actually been said about AJ – I knew he'd worked hard to overcome the obstacles. I decided to compile two lists - negative comments and positive comments. The lists filled 5 sides of A4 paper. I copy typed the ones that resonated on to individual sheets of paper.

I got mad when I read those lists and went off on another writing jag – venting my feelings on paper. Here was an individual who couldn't listen, write well or spell. He lacked concentration and made mistakes. His written work was messy and poorly presented. Many would think (on reading the reports) that he didn't apply himself, wasn't committed, goofed off and wasn't too bright. And yet within all of this lay the hidden gems. He was positive, cheerful, lively, a contributor. He had sense and sensitivity and great leadership skills (making Head of House in his final year). He was generous, caring, humorous, influential, open and honest. He was respected. Whilst all of the negatives were true, they were only true in relation to academic study. It really was 'all academic' in the larger picture of the whole person.

The next question was how to depict all of this visually. Once again I chose to free associate, this time around the headings 'symbols of academia' and 'symbols of academic struggle' (see below right). At one stage I began to think about Pink Floyd's 'The Wall' – the scene where the teachers turn into advancing rows of claw-head hammers. The children chant "Teacher! Leave them kids alone". I had to keep parking this thought as I didn't (and still don't), feel able to compete with Gerald Scarfe - the satirical cartoonist who created the imagery for the film. However, it did get me thinking about the word 'systematic' and other images came to mind; 'sausage factory', 'production line' and 'conveyor belt'. This is what the education system seemed to be about.

Extracting out the positives and negatives from AJ's school reports

I went off on a writing jag

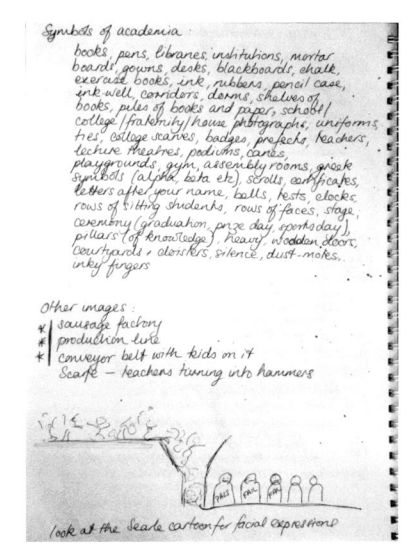

Free association around the 'symbols of academia'

Finding Your Own Visual Language | 51

I brainstormed more ideas on paper. More writing. Thoughts on colour (school uniforms), textures (blackboards covered in dust), scale of the possible pieces (landscape long and thin, like a production line) and so forth. I didn't want things to be too obvious and was hesitant about using literal imagery such as children or the human form. The phrase "they come in all shapes and sizes" seemed appropriate for kids so I doodled rough shapes in my sketchbook, along with ideas of how these capering 'things' could get processed and standardized by the system

At the end I had five different ideas of ways to advance the theme, so I began with the simplest: two pieces – one covering the positive comments of AJ's reports, the other covering the negatives. But even simple ideas can be hard to execute. It took 8 meters of experimentation to get what I wanted. Eventually I chose black linen, discharge paste and fabric paints, handwriting the comments using a needle-nosed bottle. To identify the theme of each piece I chose the simplest academic symbols – a cross for negatives and a tick/checkmark for positives.

Finally, I was satisfied. Two long, thin pieces which, though similar visually, contained very different content. I'd asked AJ for permission to use his reports. When he first saw the pieces, he fell silent before saying it was a horrible reminder of some of the worst bits of school. But, never before had he appreciated the degree of fondness, respect and liking (some) teachers had felt for him. Truly, the positives had become buried in the negatives.

Since then I've made two more pieces in this series, 'Academic Void' (shown below) and 'Square Pegs, Round Holes' (shown on page 43). I'm still working on another piece for the 'processing' idea. Three 'failures' in, I've contemplated and brainstormed new ways forward and developed new, simpler imagery. It will happen.

And what about AJ? In case you're wondering, he's made it. Runs his own small business, happily married with a family. So much for his school report. It's all academic.

One of the final pieces showing the positive aspects of AJ's school reports ('It's all Academic: Different Ability')

'Academic Void', the fourth in the series. It contains extracts from Claire's school reports

Detail of 'It's all Academic: Negative Attributes'

52 | Finding Your Own Visual Language

Case Study 2 - 'Water' **Jane Dunnewold**

I'd had in mind a series on water for a long time. Water is increasingly valuable on the planet. In some circles it's already a tradable commodity. Water purity can save lives. Lack of water can end them. We experience a drought in south Texas every summer and are put on water rationing, which even affects how much dyeing I can do with a clear conscience. I didn't know where the concept of water would take me, but most of the time we don't know where an idea will lead until we begin to explore it.

Whenever I start exploring a new theme I do some free association as I find it a useful and productive way to generate ideas and key words. My list started with the word 'water' and ran the gamut from 'wet' to 'sustaining', with a whole lot in between.

After the free association exercise was complete I studied it, seeking two things. First, words that were already representational. Images like bubbles, river, bucket and hose could be used as design elements if I felt they worked with my overall intent for the series. In truth, I didn't know yet what I wanted to express. I did know that I could focus on specific messages and meaning as I continued to explore imagery – recording my thoughts and ideas and refining them as I gathered information. However, I already knew I wouldn't use images like buckets and hoses. What I had in mind was more abstract – I didn't want to tell the whole story. I generally prefer to combine images and colors so the viewer is invited to interact with the work, projecting their ideas onto it.

My next step was to play with some of the words on my list that weren't representational. Playtime trial and error – some of my experiments were successful, some weren't. In the back of my mind I knew it would be useful to create some textural designs that would reference water, because I like to use them behind design elements printed in the foreground. I began by exploring the words waves, rolling, energizing, buoyant, expansive…

- First, I used India ink and a wide brush. I rejected the image as it didn't look like water at all. Grassy maybe, but not watery.
- Next, I tried doing sweeping strokes with the brush. This was better, but the circle didn't make sense – I couldn't connect circles and water in my mind (although it would be great for a 'circle/round/wholeness' theme!).
- Finally I got a strong image I could identify with. I got it by photocopying the 'rejected' circle onto several clear transparencies. I cut the transparencies up and re-assembled them into a broader, more thunderous wave form.
- So far, my favorite image is the one shown bottom right, also made by cutting up transparencies and reassembling them. It captures the power of the ocean and waves. It's more representational than I originally wanted, but I'll set it aside and keep working. It may or may not make the final cut.

India ink and a wide brush; rejected because it didn't look like water. Grassy maybe, but not watery

Sweeping strokes with the brush. Better but the circle didn't make sense

I got this by photocopying the rejected circle on to several clear transparencies, cutting them up and reassembling them into a wave

Finding Your Own Visual Language | 53

I scattered shells, stones and beach glass on to the scanner and used the photocopier to change the image to black and white

Water and soap in a zip-lock bag, ready to photocopy. The clearness of the bubbles surprised me

To mimic bubbles, I used black paint, a toothbrush and a wire screen. I know this could be better

I liked what was happening with the ocean/wave imagery but was determined to work on more ephemeral water-themed imagery. Approaching it from another angle I scattered shells, stones and beach glass on my scanner…

- I scanned my arrangement using the color copy feature.
- Next, I used the copier to change the color image into black and white.
- Then I enlarged parts of the black & white image and while I was still mulling over the results, I felt the patterns on the shells had potential.
- If I continued to explore the patterns I'd either draw them with India ink or continue to enlarge them on the copier. If enlarged enough, the patterns would no longer resemble shells. Instead, they would be isolated patterns or textures.

Thinking about patterns and texture led my mind to symbolic considerations. If the seas are threatened and the shells and sea-life diminishing, could environmental devastation lead to a time when the patterning and beauty of the shells no longer existed? Something to chew on.

The copier is useful so I thought I'd try another abstraction. What about bubbles? How to get bubbles to copy?

- I put a small amount of water in a zip-lock bag with some soap.
- I shook the bag to create the bubbles and then laid it on the copier glass (double-checking that the bag was tightly closed).
- I was surprised at how clearly the bubbles appeared in the photocopy.
- To mimic them, I used black paint, a toothbrush and a wire screen. But I wasn't satisfied with this image and knew it could be better. Maybe I could draw bubbles using India ink, maybe a black and white photocopy? I still need to work on this but the image is moving closer to what I see in my mind's eye.

So, I'm working toward my water series and enjoying what's coming out, but it isn't there yet, which is an important aspect of the process to acknowledge. Ideas and themes don't come fully formed. It may take months or even years to reach a point at which you have enough information and impetus to start the actual creation of works.

***Right:* Two panels of a set of four, titled 'Quartet: Water', by Jane Dunnewold. Images were first copied onto archival canvas using the laser printer and then collaged with screen printing, organza, paint and colored pencil. Each image is 10" x 10" stretched on to a 1" deep frame**

The earth is seventy percent water. Human beings are also seventy pe...

The Writing Exercises

Introduction

In our collective experience, writing equals articulation. Writing with a purpose reveals relationships, which lead to strategies for making the work.

The exercises contained in this chapter aren't designed to replace any journaling you may do. A journal is a separate discipline, but as is true with journaling, your writing will not (necessarily) be shared with anyone. Writing can be for your use only. This isn't because anything you write is going to be particularly crazy or scary - in fact, most of the exercises are stimulating and uplifting to do and some can be cathartic. However, writing stuff down does make some people feel odd, so this assurance is meant to encourage you to approach the idea of writing openly and enthusiastically. But if you wish to share things with a group, a tutor, a partner or a friend, do so.

Decide if you're going to write in a notebook/sketchbook, on the computer, or both. If you use a notebook, get something you'll feel free to tear pages from, or use photocopy paper that you could put in some kind of binder with other references.

Choose a place and time that minimizes distractions. Background music can be combined with writing, although this varies from person to person. Feel comfortable within the space you've chosen. As with the visual activities described in the 'Getting Started' chapter, there are more writing activities given here than you need to complete. Start with something that appeals to you. Try not to be tempted to stop and read what you've written – just write without judgment or expectation. Trust the power of articulating your thoughts to stimulate additional ideas, many of which will lead to the development of powerful imagery and ultimately, powerful work.

Supplies

Simple. All you'll need is a notebook and pen or a computer and a printer. A place that's comfortable and free from distraction. And time.

Writing Exercise 1
Free Association

Free association requires the use of a single word as a trigger. Allow your unconscious to respond by suspending thought and holding back judgment. Free association is a very useful activity leading to ideas or imagery you wouldn't necessarily discover another way.

Step 1
- Choose at least one word related to your topic, theme or idea.
- Write this word at the top of an empty sheet of paper.
- Set a timer for 1 minute.
- Now look at the word and write down whatever comes into your head.
- Keep writing until either your timer buzzes and says 'stop' or if you're in full flow, until your associations dry up.

Step 2
- You now have a list of words.
- Review the list and without thinking, mark or highlight the words that resonate with you.
- Write this 'shortlist' in columns across a new sheet of paper.
- Take each word one at a time and free associate again. Try not to be distracted by what's coming in the next column, and don't worry if the same words repeat themselves across the columns. If you need separate sheets of paper that's okay too.
- Look at the lists. Highlight words that repeat in more than one column – repetition means they're important, so pay attention to them.
- Look at the lists and once again, mark or highlight the words that resonate or strike you as valuable.
- Consider the lists and look for literal, visual imagery. In the example shown on the right we can see 'bars', 'coils' etc. This kind of literal imagery can be used as a springboard for the visual activities in the 'Getting Started' chapter. Other words in the example may help develop imagery - such as 'sharp', 'cruel' or 'pointed'.
- You can also look at the words and think about the colours you associate with them.

Step 3
- When you have a list of key words, use them as the basis for visual exercises as a way to expand upon them.

Writing Exercise 2
Letter Writing

Letter writing generates 'editorial' content instead of lists. It can mimic a conversation you might have with a friend or allow you to go off on a rant without upsetting anyone (see Claire's example on page 51).

Step 1
- Write down a key word or brief heading that describes your topic.
- You're now going to write yourself a letter about that topic. If writing to yourself seems weird, then pretend you're writing a letter to a very close friend (one who'll relish the ideas and ignore poor grammar, structure or spelling!).
- Don't procrastinate or start analyzing. Just get on with it. Whatever you write is fine, and one thought often leads to the next even though you don't know where the whole thing is headed. Write until you're finished. Then stop.

Step 2
- Review what you've written, highlight/mark words or concepts that resonate or appear and reappear.
- Do whatever seems best for you next - free association around key words, sketching of ideas, undertaking imagery exercises and so forth.

An example of free association. The words 'hook, barbed/razor wire, hunted, net, caged and fenced in' came as a result of a previous free association on the word 'trapped'

Finding Your Own Visual Language

Writing Exercise 3
Location Writing

Think about different environments such as;

- The natural world - the countryside, a national park, a forest, a lakeshore, a beach.
- A 'human-made' environment - cities, towns, shopping centers, supermarkets, railway stations, churches, museums, building sites etc.

Step 1
- Pick an environment that's special to you or appropriate. It could be a place you love but for a change, don't discount writing in a place that challenges you.
- If you can, go to that place with a notebook (or laptop if you prefer).
- Walk about, stand and look, sit down. Breathe it in. Absorb it.
- Write down your thoughts and feelings.

Step 2
- Review what you've written, highlight/mark words or concepts that resonate or that crop up again and again.
- Move on to do whatever seems best for you next - free association around key words, sketch out ideas, undertake imagery exercises and so forth.

Louise does some location writing

Writing Exercise 4
Visualising

Visualising is an activity that is effective across many disciplines. Athletes are encouraged to visualise winning. Climbers envision reaching the top of the mountain. Chefs see the dish on the plate. Have a go at visualising your topic – not the finished piece necessarily, just the topic.

Step 1
- Find a comfortable place; it could be anywhere (as with Location Writing).
- Sit, stand, or lie down - whatever feels comfortable.
- Close your eyes. Breathe deeply. This is a kind of meditation: "you don't need eyes to see, you need vision" (Maxi Jazz, musician, singer and songwriter).
- Now think about your topic and try to see it. Spend between 2 and 5 minutes doing this. Try to pay attention to small details.
- Wake yourself up and write about what you saw in as much detail as possible; colors, shapes and compositional elements are examples of the visual information gleaned by the exercise.

Step 2
- Review what you've written, highlight/mark words or concepts that resonate or that crop up repeatedly.
- Choose another activity - free association around key words, sketching ideas, imagery exercises and so forth.

Variations on the Theme
Instead of writing about what you visualised, try to sketch it in full, glorious color.

58 | Finding Your Own Visual Language

Writing Exercise 5
Questioning

If you've clarified your subject matter through activities such as Free Association or Letter Writing, it can help to develop a set of questions to further focus images related to your topic.

Step 1
- Devise a list of questions. For example:
  1. What's it all about?
  2. Where did it come from?
  3. What is it specifically that's resonating with me? Why is it important?
  4. How does it make me feel?
  5. What does it make me think?

Step 2
- Answer the questions using a list format or as a letter/article.

Step 3
- Review what you've written, highlight/mark words or concepts that resonate or that crop up again and again.
- Continue to refine ideas by using free association to key words, sketching ideas, undertaking imagery exercises and so forth.

Writing Exercise 6
Colour Free Association

This is similar to free associating around an idea/concept/source but this time the activity is based on colour.

- Write down a colour at the top of the page.
- Set the timer for one minute.
- Write down words that spring to mind – don't judge or evaluate. Keep writing words as long as you can, or until the timer rings.
- Study the list to determine your own, personal colour symbolism, which is an aspect of your development of a personal visual language.

If you complete this exercise and continue by working around the colour wheel, you'll have determined your colour language. This is extremely useful when you reach the stage of actually planning artwork, as you'll already know what colours to use to propel your visual story forward.

Try picking a colour from this picture as the basis for your colour free association

Finding Your Own Visual Language | 59

Writing Exercise 7
What's Emerging?

This exercise acts as a review activity for both the written and visual exercises. If the design work you've done was without any specific topic in mind, your subconscious may have spoken. This can mean that a theme, story or message may have surfaced through your writing or your imagery. If you've worked with a specific topic in mind, this exercise helps identify connections and storylines.

So, take some time out. Go back and read what you've written or look at your imagery. Pay particular attention to:

- The same or similar words/images repeating. Count the number of times they appear or highlight/isolate them.
- Links between words and images. If a link exists, start "bundling" images and words together on a separate page, or start a new file/box.
- Look for specific clues that could lead to developing more imagery or compositional ideas.
- What other exercises could you do to help develop your concept/idea?

There are many ways of working, as Tiggy discovers

Louise takes stock

And Finally - Re-Visit & Keep Working

Finding your own visual language is an ongoing process. As you become comfortable with the design process you'll pinpoint activities that work best for you. You'll also adapt techniques to suit your own style, or you'll invent new activities and ways of developing your language.

As an ongoing investment in your process consider:

- Starting a new 'box' related to your topic or concept or just to gather fodder for the future.
- Do research on the web, read books, be aware of potential sources of ideas.
- Look back at your existing imagery - look for repeats, similarities, connections, images that resonate. If you start on a new subject you may have materials in the files that can be used, developed or act as triggers.
- Look for personal symbols and do further work to truly claim them.
- Work at abstraction.
- Claim universal symbols as your own if they're important to you.

Above all, try to think laterally. Adapt and tweak the exercises in this book. Create new ones of your own. Developing a surer artistic voice is a bit like developing a fit body – you have to do the work! Artists aren't (generally) visited by Divine Inspiration. It doesn't 'just happen'. Singers sing. Writers write. Dancers dance. Athletes train. Gardeners plant. Chefs cook. Pilots fly. Musicians play. Artists practice.

And sometimes, you just have to trust the process. To quote Ronald Pearsall (Painting Abstract Pictures, David & Charles 1991):

"Sometimes, even artists aren't aware of what they're doing; they only know that they have to paint a picture a certain way. They have no conscious colour schemes; the colours on their canvas just arrive. Sometimes however they are fully aware: their pictures have been thought about, the elements balanced with mathematical skill. Will this circle match this rectangle? Is this particular colour too strong? Will this patch of black take the eye out of the picture?

Some are interested in making decorations, finding joy in arranging shapes and colours, knowing that someone else will like them too. Others are intent on exploring the nature of things, creating visual equivalents of almost anything - moods, half remembered dreams, sensations ...".

To be a practicing artist is to practice. Get started. Today. Now. And enjoy the journey.

Finding Your Own Visual Language | 61

Resources/Suppliers

Art Van Go
The Studios, 1 Stevenage Road, Knebworth, Herts G3 6AN
Telephone: 01438 814946
www.artvango.co.uk
Shop, van and mail-order.

Atlantis Art
7-9 Plumber's Road, London E1 1EQ
020 7377 8855
www.atlantisart.co.uk
The retail warehouse is in London but the catalogue is on-line and you can mail-order through an email order form.

Dick Blick
PO Box 1267, Galesburgh, IL 61402, U.S.A.
www.dickblick.com
A huge arts and craft mail order company.

Great Art
01420 593 332
www.greatart.co.uk
A German-based company with a distribution centre in the UK. Mail order.

Jacksons Art Supplies
0870 241 1849
www.jacksonsart.co.uk
A London-based company who also mail order.

Arch 66, Station Approach, Fulham, London SW6 3UH
020 7384 3055

1 Farleigh Place, London N16 7SX
020 7254 0077

Patchwork Shop/PDPM
85649 Otterloh, Hauptstr. 7a. Germany
+49-(0)89-67 73 26
www.patchworkshop.de or www.pdpm.de
Whilst Guenther specialises in suppies for textile artists, his online offering offers much more. He speaks excellent English, so don't be afraid to email him.

Thermofax Screens
Foxley Farm, Foxley, Towcester NN12 8HP
www.thermofaxscreens.co.uk
Claire Higgott runs this mail order thermofax service. She will turn your designs into screens ready for you to print finely detailed or textural marks onto cloth or paper. You simply send photocopies or email your artwork and she does the rest. Email Claire for details of screen sizes and prices.

*Left: Crystallographic balance
(Charlie Monckton & Sal Spring,
'Missing the Point: Juicy', detail)*

Further Reading

We've sorted books according to interest. If you want to pursue a particular field with the ideas we've proposed, choose additional reading from the categories below.

Journaling, Philosophy, Design

- Adams, Kathleen; *Journal to the Self*. Time Warner Books. New York. 1990.
- Baldwin, Christina; *Life's Companion*: Journal Writing as a Spiritual Quest. Bantam Books. New York. 1991.
- Bayles, David and Orland, Ted. *Art & Fear*. The Image Continuum. Santa Cruz, CA and Eugene, Or. 1993.
- Capacchione, Lucia; *Healing Your Life with Art*. Hay House, Inc. Santa Monica, CA. 1990.
- Capacchione, Lucia; *The Creative Journal*: The Art of Finding Yourself. Swallow Press. Akron, Ohio. 1979.
- Chicago, Judy; *Through the Flower*. Anchor Doubleday. 1977.
- Exploratorium, The (Murphy, Pat, Neill, William); *By Nature's Design*. Chronicle Books, San Francisco, Ca. 1993
- Exploratorium, The (Pat Murphy & Paul Doherty); *The Color of Nature*. Chronicle Books, San Francisco, CA. 1996.
- Flack, Audrey; *Art and Soul*: Notes on Creating. EP Dutton. 1986.
- Fletcher, Alan; *Picturing and Poeting*. Phaidon Press Ltd. London, UK. 2006.
- Fletcher, Alan; *Beware Wet Paint*. Phaidon Press Ltd. London, UK. 1994.
- Fletcher, Alan; *The Art of Looking Sideways*. Phaidon Press Ltd. London, UK. 2001.
- Garnett, Lynne; *Finding the Great Creative You*. Aslan Publishing. Boulder Creek, CO. 1990.
- Gerber, Anna; *All Messed Up (unpredictable graphics)*. Laurence King Publishing. London, UK. 2004.
- Goldberg, Natalie; *Writing Down the Bones*. Shambhala Inc. Boston & London. 1986.
- Jung, Carl; *Memories, Dreams and Reflections*. Vintage Books. 1965.
- McNiff, Shaun; *Trust the Process*. Shambhala Inc. Boston & London. 1996.
- Nin, Anais; *Diaries* (several volumes), assorted printings.
- Prather, Hugh; *Notes to Myself*. Bantam. 1979.
- Anne Truitt; *Daybook - The Journal of an Artist*. Penguin. 1982.

Surface Design

- Benn, Claire, and Morgan, Leslie; *Tray Dyeing*. Self published. Committed to Cloth. United Kingdom. 2006.
- Benn, Claire, and Morgan, Leslie; *Breakdown Printing*. Self published. Committed to Cloth. United Kingdom. 2005.
- Brackman, Holly; The Surface Designer's Handbook: Dyeing, Printing, Painting and Creating Resists on Fabric. Interweave Press, 2006
- Dunnewold, Jane; *Complex Cloth*. Bothell, WA. Fiber Studio Press, 1996.
- Dunnewold, Jane; *Improvisational Screen Printing*. Self-published. San Antonio, TX. 2003.
- Dunnewold, Jane; *The CD & DVD Resource* (various titles). Self published. Art Cloth Studios. San Antonio, TX. 2005 and on-going.
- Issett, Ruth; *Colour on Paper & Fabric*. Batsford, 2000.
- Johnston, Ann; *Dye Painting!* Paducah, KY. American Quilter's Society. 1992.
- Johnston, Ann; *Color By Accident*. Self-published. Lake Oswego, OR. 1997
- Johnston, Ann; *Color By Design*. Self-published. Lake Oswego, OR. 2000.
- Knutson, Linda; *Synthetic Dyes for Natural Fibers*. Seattle. Madrona Press, 1982.
- Laury, Jean Ray; *Imagery on Fabric*. Lafayette, CA. C&T Publishing, 1992.
- Noble, Elin; *Paints and Dyes*. Bothell, WA. Fiber Studio Press, 1998. Also re-issued as a self-published book in 2002
- Page, Gloria; *Art Stamping Workshop*. Cincinnati, Ohio. North Light Books. 2006.
- Wells, Kate; *Fabric Dyeing and Printing*. Loveland, CO. Interweave Press. 1997.

Embroidery and Stitching

- Beaney, Jan, and Littlejohn, Jean. These authors have written an entire series of inspiring books on contemporary stitching and embroidery. Their titles can be ordered from Double Trouble Enterprises and as an example include:

  A Tale of Two Stitches
  A Sketch in Time
  Bonding and Beyond
  Vanishing Act
  Transfer to Transform

- Beaney, Jan, and Littlejohn, Jean; *A Complete Guide to Creative Embroidery*. London. Batsford Reprint 1997.
- Enthoven, Jacquiline; *The Stitches of Creative Embroidery*. New York. Van Nostrand Reinhold Company. 1964. Reprinted in the 1980's. The all time clearest book to use for learning stitches.
- The Embroiderer's Guild; *Embroidery Studio*. Newton, Abbot Devon. David & Charles. 1997.

Finding Your Own Visual Language | 63

About Us

Art Cloth Studios

Jane Dunnewold is the author of the seminal book 'Complex Cloth' (Fiber Studio Press, 1996). Jane loves to teach and is certain that teaching feeds her own work. She shares everything she knows and wants her students to as good as, and even better, than she is as an artist. One of her chief tasks in life as a teacher is to help students sort out the ethical issues while learning artistic process. Learning to do something well, learning to work from your own designs with tools that you've made yourself (rather than commercial ones) are important. She feels that ultimately, students will claim the tools and processes as their own and as a result, develop their own style and voice.

Committed to Cloth

Committed to Cloth is a partnership between Leslie Morgan & Claire Benn, formed in 2000 as a result of a shared love of textiles, wet work, stitch and construction. Claire and Leslie are practising artists who also love to teach as "to teach is to learn twice". Neither Claire or Leslie care how cloth is used as long as it provides the creative output for those choosing to use it. Cloth is tactile, cloth is flexible and doesn't mind what's done to it. They want people to learn, develop, grow and most importantly, have fun and enjoy their work with cloth and stitch.

PUBLICATIONS FROM ART CLOTH STUDIO AND/OR COMMITTED TO CLOTH

We enjoy sharing knowledge, so check the websites from time to time to find out what's new on our list. To date, other titles include;

Art Cloth Studio titles (www.artclothstudios.com)

Improvisational Screen Printing
Complex Cloth - The Workshops
Paper and Metal Leaf Lamination
Multi-Coloured Printing with an Interfacing Stencil
Edges & Borders: Innovative Finishing Techniques for Textiles
Disciple of Life
Never Static
The Girl's Guide to Life

Committed to Cloth titles (www.committedtocloth.com)

Breakdown Printing; new dimensions in texture & colour
Tray Dyeing; exploring colour, texture and special effects

Right: 'Shooting the Past', Claire Higgott